A Bundle of Laughs

A Bundle of Laughs

J. John & Mark Stibbe

MONARCH
BOOKS

Oxford, UK & Grand Rapids, Michigan, USA

First published in the UK in 2005 by Monarch Books
(a publishing imprint of Lion Hudson plc),
Mayfield House, 256 Banbury Road, Oxford OX2 7DH
Tel: +44 (0) 1865 302750 Fax: +44 (0) 1865 302757
Email: monarch@lionhudson.com
www.lionhudson.com

Reprinted 2005, 2007

Cover illustration by Rosie Brooks
Illustrations by Darren Harvey Regan

Distributed by:
UK: Marston Book Services Ltd, PO Box 269,
Abingdon, Oxon OX14 4YN
USA: Kregel Publications, PO Box 2607,
Grand Rapids, Michigan 49501

ISBN: 978 1 85424 686 8 (UK)
ISBN: 978 0 8254 6079 1 (USA)

The text paper used in this book has been made from wood independently
certified as having come from sustainable forests.

British Library Cataloguing Data
A catalogue record for this book is available
from the British Library.

Printed and bound in Malta by Gutenberg Press

Note to church magazine editors

Permission to use up to 750 words from this volume is granted free of charge for reproduction in church magazines when produced on a non-commercial basis. Please acknowledge source in the following form: From *A Bundle of Laughs*, J. John and Mark Stibbe, Monarch Books.

Dedication

Dedicated to the people of St Andrew's Church, Chorleywood, who have been the guinea pigs for the material in this book and the previous three volumes.

ACCOUNTABILITY

A rabbi was walking home when he noticed a congregant walking ahead of him. The rabbi hurried to catch up as he had some important matters to discuss. Much to his dismay he saw that the congregant had entered a "rib joint". The rabbi couldn't believe his eyes!

He looked again and saw the congregant pointing to the menu and talking to the waiter. He looked again and saw the waiter deliver a slab of pork ribs to the congregant.

Then the rabbi, with his nose pressed to the window, saw the congregant take the ribs and start eating the non-kosher meal. The rabbi could no longer contain himself. He burst into the restaurant and said, "Moshe, what are you doing?"

Moshe looked up and said to the rabbi, "I don't understand."

The rabbi said, "I just saw you, Moshe, one of my most holy congregants, with all this non-kosher food!"

Moshe asked, "Rabbi, did you see me come into this restaurant?"

"Yes, I did!" replied the rabbi.

"Did you see me order the food?"

"Yes, I did!" replied the rabbi.

"Did you see me eat the food?"

"Of course I did! Why do you think I'm here?"

"Well then," said Moshe, "I don't see what the problem is… It was all done under rabbinical supervision."

ACTION

The person who rows the boat generally doesn't have time to rock it.

"Chop your own wood, and it will warm you twice."
Henry Ford

"To do nothing is in every man's power."
Samuel Johnson

"A life spent making mistakes is not only more honourable, but more useful than a life spent doing nothing."
George Bernard Shaw

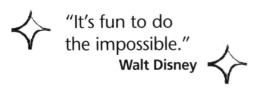

The best angle to approach a problem from is the try angle.

"It's fun to do the impossible."
Walt Disney

"Even if you're on the right track, you'll get run over if you just sit there!"
Will Rogers

"Things may come to those who wait, but only the things left by those who hustle."
Abraham Lincoln

"Well done is better than well said."
Benjamin Franklin

"It is better to begin in the evening than not at all."
English proverb

In the *Star Wars* sequel, *The Empire Strikes Back*, Yoda – the Jedi teacher – tries to implant in Luke Skywalker the means of engaging the Force that is the greatest power in the universe. He says to his pupil, "Luke, there is no TRY; there is either DO or NOT DO."

ADVERTS

The following were actually taken from classified ads in newspapers:

Free Yorkshire terrier. Eight years old. Hateful little dog

**Free puppies: half Cocker Spaniel –
half sneaky neighbour's dog**

Free puppies: part German Shepherd – part stupid dog

Snow blower for sale: only used on snowy days

***2 wire-mesh butchering gloves:
one five-finger, one three-finger. Pair: £10***

*"Tickle me" Elmo, still in box, comes with its own 1988 Mustang,
5L, auto, excellent condition: £4,000*

Hummels – largest selection ever.
"If it's in stock, we have it!"

Nice parachute: never opened – used once

Tired of working for only $9.75 per hour? We offer profit-sharing and flexible hours. Starting pay: $7–$9 per hour

Our sofa will seat the whole mob. 100% Italian leather

Joining nudist colony! Selling washer and dryer: £200

FOR SALE BY OWNER: complete set of *Encyclopedia Britannica* – 45 volumes, excellent condition: £700. No longer needed. Recently married; wife knows everything.

SUPER GRANNY – DEFENDER OF JUSTICE

The following is a true story reported in *USA Today*:

An elderly Florida lady did her shopping, and upon returning to her car, she found four males in the act of leaving with her vehicle. She dropped her shopping bags and drew her handgun, proceeding to scream at the top of her voice, "I have a gun, and I know how to use it! Get out of the car!"

The four men didn't wait for a second invitation. They got out and ran like mad. The lady, somewhat shaken, then proceeded to load her shopping bags into the back of the car and get into the driver's seat. She was so shaken that she could not get her key into the ignition.

She tried and tried, and then it dawned on her why. A few minutes later she found her own car parked four or five spaces further down. She loaded her bags into the car and then drove to the police station.

The sergeant to whom she told the story doubled over on the floor with laughter. He pointed to the other end of the counter, where four pale men were reporting a car-jacking by a mad, elderly woman described as white, less than five feet tall, with glasses and curly white hair, and carrying a large handgun.

No charges were filed.

"You can live to be a hundred, if you give up all the things that make you want to live to be a hundred."
Woody Allen

Middle age is when broadness of the mind and narrowness of the waist change places.

"You know you've reached middle age when your weightlifting consists of merely standing up."
Bob Hope

"It is never too late to be who you might have been."
George Eliot

"You know you're old when you've lost all your marvels."
Merry Browne

"Grey hair is God's graffiti."
Bill Cosby

"Anyone who stops learning is old, whether at 20 or 80."
Henry Ford

"Old age ain't no place for sissies."
Bette Davis

"As you grow older, you'll find the only things you regret are the things you didn't do."
Zachary Scott

"Old age is not so bad when you consider the alternatives."
Maurice Chevalier

You know you are getting old when you tend to repeat yourself. You know you are getting old when you tend to repeat yourself.

"Life would be infinitely happier if we could only be born at the age of 80 and gradually approach 18."
Mark Twain

God, keep my heart attuned to laughter
When my youth is done;
When all the days are grey days, coming after
The warmth, the sun.
God, keep me then from bitterness, from grieving,
When my life seems cold;
God, keep me always loving and believing,
As I grow old.

ANGER

Some people are like buttons; they pop off at the wrong time.

No man can think clearly when his fists are clenched.

George Nathan

For every minute you are angry, you lose 60 seconds of happiness.

"Not even the fastest horse can catch a word spoken in anger."

Chinese proverb

"If you are patient in one moment of anger, you will avoid 100 days of sorrow."

Chinese proverb

"Speak when you are angry and you will make the best speech you will ever regret."

Ambrose Bierce

ANGLICANISM

A billionaire had three sons and as it was coming up to Christmas he was wondering what to buy them.

The first son said, "Daddy, Daddy, I really love flying; I just can't spend enough time in the air." So his dad bought him a 747.

The second son said, "All I want to do is improve my golf handicap." So Dad bought him a golf course.

The third son said, "All I want is a cowboy outfit." So Daddy bought him the Church of England.

ANIMALS

A man and his dog were walking along a road. The man was enjoying the scenery, when it suddenly occurred to him that he was dead. He remembered dying, and he realised the dog walking beside him had been dead for years. He wondered where the road was leading them. After a while, they came to a high, white stone wall along one side of the road. It looked like marble. At the top of a long hill, it was broken by a tall arch that glowed in the sunlight.

When he was standing before it he saw a magnificent gate in the arch that looked like mother-of-pearl; and the street that led to the gate looked like pure gold. He and the dog walked towards the gate, and as he got closer, he saw a man at a desk to one side.

When he was close enough, he called out, "Excuse me, where are we?"

"This is heaven, sir," the man answered.

"Wow!" said the traveller. "Would you happen to have some water?"

"Of course, sir. Come right in, and I'll have some iced water brought right up." The man at the desk gestured, and the gate began to open.

"Can my friend come in too?" the traveller asked, gesturing towards his dog.

"I'm sorry, sir, but we don't accept pets."

The man thought for a

moment and then turned back towards the road and continued the way he had been going with his dog. After another long walk and at the top of another long hill, he came to a dirt road that led through a farm gate that looked as if it had never been closed. There was no fence.

As he approached the gate, he saw a man inside, leaning against a tree and reading a book.

"Excuse me!" he called to the reader. "Do you have any water?"

"Yeah, sure, there's a pump over there." The man pointed to a place that couldn't be seen from outside the gate. "Come on in."

"How about my friend here?" The traveller gestured to his dog.

"There should be a bowl by the pump."

They went through the gate and, sure enough, there was an old-fashioned hand pump with a bowl beside it. The traveller filled the bowl and took a long drink himself, then gave some to the dog. When they were full, he and the dog walked back towards the man, who was standing by the tree waiting for them.

"What do you call this place?" the traveller asked.

"This is heaven," was the answer.

"Well, that's confusing," the traveller said. "The man down the road said that was heaven, too."

"Oh, you mean the place with the gold street and pearly gates? Nope. That's hell."

"Doesn't it make you mad for them to use your name like that?"

"No. I can see how you might think so, but we're just happy that they screen out the folks who'll leave their best friends behind."

APPEARANCES

Jake is struggling through a bus station with two huge and obviously heavy suitcases when a stranger walks up to him and asks, "Have you got the time?"

Jake sighs, puts down the suitcases and glances at his wrist.

"It's a quarter to six," he says.

"Hey, that's a pretty fancy watch!" exclaims the stranger.

Jake brightens a little. "Yeah, it's not bad. It's an invention of mine. Check this out." He shows the stranger a time zone display, not just for every time zone in the world, but for the 86 largest cities.

He hits a few buttons and from somewhere in the watch a voice says, "The time is ten past seven," in a west Texas accent.

He hits a few more buttons and the same voice says something in Japanese. Jake continues, "I've put in regional accents for each city."

The display is unbelievably high-quality and the voice is simply astounding, and the stranger is full of admiration.

"That's not all," says Jake. He pushes a few more buttons and a tiny but very high-resolution map of New York City appears on the display. "The flashing dot shows our location by satellite positioning," explains Jake. "You can zoom in and out as well," he adds, "and the display changes to show all of eastern New York state."

"I want to buy this watch!" says the stranger.

"Oh, no, it's not ready for sale yet. I'm still ironing out the bugs. But look at this," says Jake, as he proceeds to demonstrate that the watch is also a very creditable little FM radio receiver with a digital tuner, a sonar device that can measure distances up to 125 metres, a pager with thermal paper printout and, most impressive of all, has the capacity for voice recordings of up to 300 standard-size books.

"I only have 32 of my favourites in there so far," says Jake.

"I've got to have this watch!" says the stranger.

"No, you don't understand," argues Jake. "It's not ready yet."

"I'll give you $1,000 for it!"

"Oh, no, I've already spent more than that on it."

"I'll give you $5,000 for it!"

"But it's just not…"

"I'll give you $15,000 for it!" exclaims the stranger, pulling out a chequebook.

Jake stops to think. He's only put about $8,500 into materials and development, and with $15,000 he can make another one and have it ready for merchandising in under six months.

The stranger frantically finishes writing the cheque and waves it in front of him. "Here it is, ready to hand to you right here and now. $15,000. Take it or leave it."

Jake abruptly makes his decision. "OK," he says, and peels off the watch. They make the exchange and the stranger turns to leave.

"Hey, wait a minute!" calls Jake after the stranger, who turns around warily. Jake points to the two suitcases he'd been trying to wrestle through the bus station. "Don't forget your batteries."

"Things are not always what they seem."

Phaedrus

"All that glitters is not gold."

Cervantes

A.S.A.P.

Ever wonder about the abbreviation A.S.A.P.? Generally we think of it in terms of even more hurry and stress in our lives, but maybe if we think of this abbreviation in a different manner, we will begin to find a new way to deal with those rough days along the way.

> There's work to do, deadlines to meet;
> You've got no time to spare,
> But as you hurry and scurry –
> A.S.A.P. – ALWAYS SAY A PRAYER.
>
> In the midst of family chaos,
> "Quality time" is rare.
> Do your best; let God do the rest –
> A.S.A.P. – ALWAYS SAY A PRAYER.
>
> It may seem like your worries
> Are more than you can bear.
> Slow down and take a breather –
> A.S.A.P. – ALWAYS SAY A PRAYER.
>
> God knows how stressful life is;
> He wants to ease our cares,
> And he'll respond to all your needs
> A.S.A.P. – ALWAYS SAY A PRAYER.

ATHEISM

An atheist professor was teaching a college class. He told the students that he was going to prove that there was no God.

He said, "God, if you are real, then I want you to knock me off this platform. I'll give you fifteen minutes!"

Ten minutes went by. He kept saying, "Here I am, God. I'm still waiting…"

As he got down to the last couple of minutes, a big 240-pound football player ran up and hit the professor full force, sending him flying off the platform. The professor got up, obviously shaken, and said, "Where did *you* come from? And why did you do that?"

The football player replied, "God was busy. He sent me!"

Once upon a time there was a family of mice who lived all their lives inside a large piano. To them, in their piano world, came the music of the instrument, filling all the dark spaces with sound and harmony.

At first the mice were impressed by it. They drew comfort and wonder from the thought that there was Someone who made the music – though invisible to them – above, yet close to them. They loved to think of the Great Player whom they could not see.

Then one day, a daring mouse climbed up part of the piano and returned very thoughtful. He had found out how the music was made. Wires were the secret: tightly stretched wires of graduated lengths which trembled and vibrated. The mice must now revise all their old beliefs: none but the most conservative could any longer believe in the Unseen Player.

Later, another explorer carried the explanation further. Hammers were now the secret: numbers of hammers, dancing and leaping on the wires. This was a more complicated theory, but it all went to show that they lived in a purely mechanical and mathematical world.

The Unseen Player came to be thought of as a myth.

But the pianist continued to play.

> *"I would rather live my life as if there is a God and die to find out there isn't, than live my life as if there isn't and die to find out there is."*
>
> **Albert Camus**

ATTITUDE

A tea kettle, although up to its neck in hot water, continues to sing.

It's better to light a candle than curse the darkness.

"Those who wish to sing always find a song."
Swedish proverb

"Wherever you go, no matter what the weather, always bring your own sunshine."
Anthony J D'Angelo

Thou shalt not whine!

"A man's as miserable as he thinks he is."
Marcus Seneca

"A positive attitude may not solve all your problems, but it will annoy enough people to make it worth the effort."

Herm Albright

"I can't complain, but sometimes I still do."

Joe Walsh

"A happy person is not a person in a certain set of circumstances, but rather a person with a certain set of attitudes."

Hugh Downs

"I am not a has-been. I am a will-be."

Lauren Bacall

"We can destroy ourselves by cynicism and disillusion, just as effectively as by bombs."

Kenneth Clark

"Since the house is on fire let us warm ourselves."

Italian proverb

"We're all in the gutter, but some of us are looking at the stars."

Oscar Wilde

"Happiness is an attitude. We either make ourselves miserable, or happy and strong. The amount of work is the same."

Francesca Reigler

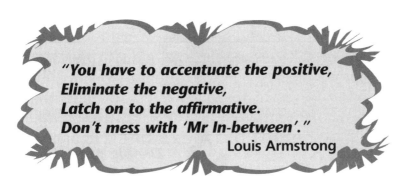

"You have to accentuate the positive,
Eliminate the negative,
Latch on to the affirmative.
Don't mess with 'Mr In-between'."
Louis Armstrong

"Keep a green tree in your heart and perhaps a singing bird will come."

Chinese proverb

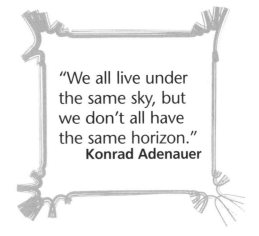

"We all live under the same sky, but we don't all have the same horizon."
Konrad Adenauer

Attitudes are contagious.
Is yours worth catching?

BALDNESS

Real men don't waste their hormones growing hair.

God is good, God is fair;
To some he gave brains,
To others hair!

God made just so many perfect heads; the rest he covered with hair.

The big advantage of being bald is that you can style your hair with a damp cloth!

Grey hair is a blessing – ask any bald man.

This is not a bald spot – it's a solar panel for brain power!

BAPTISTS

A woman called a Baptist minister and asked him if he would take a funeral for her dog who had died.

"I can't do that, ma'am," he said. "Why don't you try the Methodist preacher?"

"All right," she replied, "but can you give me some advice? How much should I pay him? $300 or $400?"

"Hold on," he said. "I didn't know your dog was a Baptist."

A Methodist pastor says to a Baptist pastor, "If I immerse somebody just up to his ankles, it that enough?"

"No," answers the Baptist.

"How about up to his knees?"

"Nope."

"How about up to his shoulders?"

"No, sir!"

"You mean I've got to get the water over the top of his head?"

"That's right," says the Baptist.

"Good," says the Methodist. "That proves that it's the top of the head that's the important part to get wet and that's what we do – sprinkle the head."

BEAUTY

"Science will never be able to reduce the value of a sunset to arithmetic. Nor can it reduce friendship to a formula. Laughter and love, pain and loneliness, the challenge of beauty and truth: these will always surpass the scientific mastery of nature."
Louis Orr

"Anyone who keeps the ability to see beauty never grows old."
Franz Kafka

"Poetry lifts the veil from the hidden beauty of the world, and makes familiar objects be as if they were not familiar."
Percy Bysshe Shelley

"You can take no credit for beauty at 16. But if you are beautiful at 60, it will be your soul's own doing."
Marie Stopes

"A man should hear a little music, read a little poetry, and see a fine picture every day of his life, in order that worldly cares may not obliterate the sense of the beautiful which God has implanted in the human soul."
Johann Wolfgang von Goethe

"I'm tired of all this nonsense about beauty being only skin deep. That's deep enough! What do you want? An adorable pancreas?"
Jean Kerr

BIBLE

> **The Bible is greater in scope than *The Lord of the Rings*, has more adventure than *Master and Commander*, more romance than *Love Actually* and in terms of popularity and sales leaves the whole *Harry Potter* series in the shade. How can it ever be regarded as boring?!**

Famous misprints

CAMELS BIBLE In 1832 an edition of the Bible had Rebecca leaving her tent to meet Isaac with a group of, not "damsels", but "camels".

WIFE-HATER BIBLE An 1810 version read, "If any man come to me, and hate not…his own wife [instead of 'life'], he cannot be my disciple."

"SIN ON" BIBLE The first English-language Bible to be printed in Ireland, in 1716, encouraged its readers to "sin on more" rather than "sin no more".
    A similar error in 1653 had declared: "Know ye not that the unrighteous shall inherit the kingdom of God?"

THE WICKED BIBLE of 1631 reported the seventh commandment as "Thou shalt commit adultery", a mistake that infuriated King Charles. He ordered all copies destroyed and fined all printers whose hands had touched the edition.

MURDERER'S BIBLE This 19th-century faux pas had Mark 7:27 as "Let the children be killed", instead of "filled".

PLACEMAKER BIBLE A 16th-century printer had Jesus blessing the "placemakers" instead of "peacemakers". An American printer later substituted the "parable of the vinegar" for the "vineyard".

PRINTER'S BIBLE Perhaps King David was on target in a 1702 edition, which quoted him as saying, "Printers [instead of 'princes'] have persecuted me without cause."

BISHOPS

A vicar's son was asked to entertain the visiting bishop while his parents prepared the lunch. The boy asked him, "Can you tell me how you become a bishop?"

The bishop replied, "Well, first you have to go to church every Sunday, then be top pupil in Sunday School and later be best student at theological college. Then you get ordained and when you are the best vicar in the diocese you become a bishop."

"Oh, I see," said the boy, "because I heard my dad say to my mum this morning he wondered how on earth you became a bishop."

BOOKS

"People of power have no time to read; yet the people who do not read are unfit for power."
Michael Foot

"A room without books is like a body without a soul."
Cicero

"I would be the most content if my children grew up to be the kind of people who think decorating consists mostly of building enough bookshelves."
Anna Quindlen

"I have always imagined that Paradise will be a kind of library."
Jorge Luis Borges

"Buying books would be a good thing if one could also buy the time to read them in: but as a rule the purchase of books is mistaken for the appropriation of their contents."
Arthur Schopenhauer

"Wear the old coat and buy the new book."

Austin Phelps

"You can't get a cup of tea large enough or a book long enough to suit me."
C S Lewis

CHANGE

"If people had been asked in 1968 which nation would dominate the world in watchmaking during the 1990s and into the twenty-first century the answer would have been uniform: Switzerland. Why? Because Switzerland had dominated the world of watchmaking for the previous 60 years.

The Swiss made the best watches in the world and were committed to constant refinement of their expertise. It was the Swiss who came forward with the minute hand and the second hand. They led the world in discovering better ways to manufacture the gears, bearings and mainsprings of watches. They even led the way in waterproofing techniques and self-winding models. By 1968, the Swiss made 65 per cent of all watches sold in the world and laid claim to as much as 90 per cent of the profits.

By 1980, however, they had laid off thousands of watchmakers and controlled less than 10 per cent of the world market. Their profit domination dropped to less than 20 per cent. Between 1979 and 1981, 50,000 of the 62,000 Swiss watchmakers lost their jobs. Why? The Swiss had refused to consider a new development – the Quartz movement – ironically, invented by a Swiss. Because it had no mainspring or knob, it was rejected. It was too much of a paradigm shift for them to embrace. Seiko, on the other hand, accepted it and, along with a few other companies, became the leader in the watch industry.

The lesson of the Swiss watchmakers is profound. A past that was so secure, so profitable, so dominant was destroyed by an unwillingness to consider the future. It was more than not being able to make predictions – it was an inability to rethink how they did business. Past success had blinded them to the importance of seeing the implications of the changing world and to admitting that past accomplishment was no guarantee of future success.

James Enery White

A church was considering the purchase of a new chandelier. A parishioner who was unable to attend the business meeting where it was initially discussed wrote a note to the head deacon to express her opinion.

The note said simply:

I am definitely opposed to buying a new chandelier for the church, for three reasons:

1. I can't spell chandelier.
2. If we got one, who's going to play it?
3. If we've got that kind of money in the treasury, why don't we buy a new light fixture to brighten up the church?

"Everything continues in a state of rest unless it is compelled to change by forces impressed upon it."
Isaac Newton,
First Law of Motion

"It's not so much that we're afraid of change or so in love with the old ways, but it's that place in between that we fear... It's like being between trapezes. It's Linus when his blanket is in the dryer. There's nothing to hold on to."
Marilyn Ferguson

"Any change, at any time, for any reason, is to be deplored."
The Duke of Cambridge
(late 1800s)

Some people will change when they see the light. Others change only when they feel the heat.

The clerk of Abbington Presbytery, outside Philadelphia, approximately 100 years ago described five kinds of people, according to their attitudes to change:

1. Early innovators (2.6%); these run with new ideas
2. Early adaptors (13.4%); these are influenced by (1) but are not initiators
3. The slow majority (34%); the herd-followers
4. The reluctant majority (34%)
5. The antagonistic (16%); these will never change

"If you don't like something, change it; if you can't change it, change the way you think about it."

Mary Engelbreit

"All changes, even the most longed for, have their melancholy; for what we leave behind us is a part of ourselves; we must die to one life before we can enter another."

Anatole France

There are three stages people go through when confronted with change:

1. Resistance to change
2. Tolerance of change
3. Embracing the change

"Change is inevitable – except from a vending machine."

Robert C Gallagher

"All change is not growth, as all movement is not forward."

Ellen Glasgow

Those who never retract their opinions love themselves more than they love the truth.

"Life belongs to the living, and he who lives must be prepared for changes."

Goethe

When it comes to changes, people like only those that they make themselves.

"When one door of happiness closes, another opens; but often we look so long at the closed door that we do not see the one which has been opened for us."

Helen Keller

There is a time for departure even when there is no certain place to go.

CHILDREN

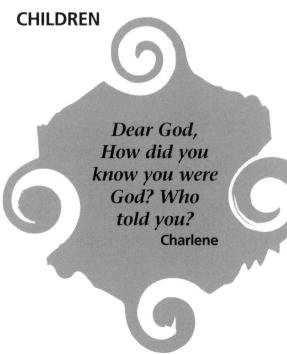

Dear God,
How did you
know you were
God? Who
told you?
Charlene

Dear God,
Thank you for the baby brother
but what I asked for was a
puppy. I never asked for anything
before. You can look it up.

Joyce

Dear God,
Please put another holiday
between Christmas and
Easter. There is nothing
good in there now.

Amanda

Dear God,
Did you really mean, Do unto others as
they do unto you? If you did, then I'm
going to get even with my brother.

Darla

Dear God,
My Grandpa says you were
around when he was a little
boy. How far back do you go?
Love,
Dennis

Dear Mr God,
I wish you would not make it so easy
for people to come apart. I had to
have three stitches and a shot.

Janet

God,
I read the Bible.
What does begat
mean? Nobody
will tell me.
Love,

Alison

Dear God,
I like the story about Noah the best of all of
them. You really made up some good ones.
I like the one about walking on water, too.

Glenn

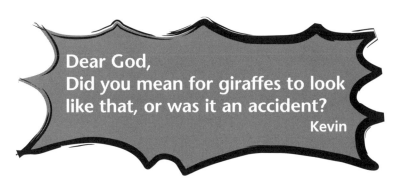

Dear God,
Did you mean for giraffes to look like that, or was it an accident?

Kevin

Dear God,
Do you draw the lines around the countries? If you don't, who does?

Norman

Dear God,
You don't have to worry about me. I always look both ways before I cross the street.

Dean

Dear God,
In school we read that Thomas Edison made light, but in Sunday School they said you did it first. Did he steal your idea?
Sincerely,

Donna

Dear God, I didn't think orange went with purple until I saw the sunset you made on Tuesday night. That was really cool.

Carol

**Dear God,
In Sunday School they told us what you do for a job. Who does it when you are on holiday?**

Jane

Dear God,
It is great the way you always get the stars in the right place. Why can't you do that with the moon?

Jeff

Dear God,
I am doing the best I can. Really.
Frank

Dear God,
What does it mean, You are a jealous God? I thought you had everything you wanted.

Jane

CHRISTIANITY

"Now that I am a Christian I do not have moods in which the whole thing looks very improbable; but when I was an atheist I had moods in which Christianity looked terribly probable."

C S Lewis

"The Christian ideal has not been tried and found wanting. It has been found difficult and left untried."

G K Chesterton

"If you love, you will suffer. And if you do not love, you do not know the meaning of the Christian life."

Agatha Christie

"Here is what Christian living entails: wishing in all things whatever God wishes; desiring his glory, seeking nothing for oneself, either now or in the hereafter."

Martin Luther

"Christianity is a battle, not a dream."

Wendell Phillips

"The purpose of Christianity is not to avoid difficulty, but to produce a character adequate to meet it when it comes. It does not make life easy; rather it tries to make us great enough for life."

James L Christensen

The world is equally shocked at hearing Christianity criticised and seeing it practised.

D Elton Trueblood

The distinction between Christianity and all other systems of religion consists largely in this, that in these others, men are found seeking after God, while Christianity is God seeking after men.

Thomas Arnold

The glory of Christianity is to conquer by forgiveness.

William Blake

Christianity helps us face the music even when we don't like the tune.

Phillips Brooks

CHRISTMAS

People who celebrate the Christian meaning of Christmas are happier than those who mark the festive season with consumer gifts, new research claims.

A report from the University of Warwick has revealed a positive relation between happiness and religion. Dr Stephen Joseph said, "Religious people seem to have a greater purpose in life, which is why they are happier. Research shows that too much materialism in our lives can be terrible for happiness."

He added, "What seems to be important is living your life in a way that emphasises the importance of being involved in your community and caring for people, and Christmas is a reminder to us all of this message."

December 2003

It's Christmas time at our house and we're putting up a tree.
I wish I could find some simple way to remember God's gift to me.

Some little sign or symbol to show friends stopping by,
The little babe was born one day but he really came to die.

Some symbol of his nail-pierced hands, the blood he shed for me.
What if I hung a nail on my Christmas tree?

I know it was his love for us that held him to a tree,
But when I see this simple nail I'll know he died for me.

It may seem strange at Christmas time to think of nails and wood,
But both were used in Jesus' life to bring us something good.

From manger bed, to crown of thorns, to death on Calvary,
God used the wood and nails of men to set all people free.

"Christmas is most truly Christmas when we celebrate it by giving the light of love to those who need it most."
Ruth Carter Stapleton

Whatever else be lost among the years,
Let us keep Christmas still a shining thing;
Whatever doubts assail us, or what fears,
Let us hold close one day, remembering
Its poignant meaning for the hearts of men;
Let us get back our childlike faith again.
Grace Noll Crowell

There was a Scottish farmer who did not believe in the Christmas story. The idea that God would become a man was absurd. His wife, however, was a devout believer and raised their children in her faith. The farmer sometimes gave her a hard time, mocking her faith and belief in the incarnation of God in the baby of Bethlehem: "It's all nonsense," he said. "Why would God lower himself to become a human like us? It's such a ridiculous story."

One snowy Sunday evening his wife took the children to church while the farmer relaxed at home. After they had left, the weather deteriorated into a blinding snowstorm. Then he heard a loud thump against the window. Then another thump! He ventured outside to see what was happening. There in the field was the strangest sight: a flock of geese! They had been migrating south but had become disorientated by the storm. They were stranded on his farm, unable to fly or to see their way.

The farmer had compassion on them. He wanted to help them and realised his barn would give them shelter for the night. He opened the barn doors and stood back, hoping they would make their way in. But they didn't realise it would be shelter for them. So he tried to shoo the geese in, but they ran in all directions. Perplexed, he got some bread and made a trail to the barn door. But they still didn't catch on. Nothing he could do would get them into the warmth and shelter of the barn.

Feeling totally frustrated, he exclaimed, "Why don't they follow me? Can't they see this is the only place where they can survive the storm? How can I possibly get them to follow me?"

He thought for a moment and then realised that they would not follow a human. He said to himself, "How can I possibly save them? The only way would be for me to become a goose. If only I could become like one of them. Then I could save them. They would follow me and I would lead them to safety."

At that moment he stopped and realised what he had said. The words reverberated in his head. "If only I could become like one of them, then I could save them." Then, at last, he understood God's heart towards humankind. He fell on his knees in the snow and worshipped him!

Monday, 8 December 2003

Please accept with no obligation, implied or implicit, our best wishes for an environmentally conscious, socially responsible, low-stress, non-addictive, gender-neutral celebration of the winter solstice holiday (or summer solstice in the southern hemisphere), practised within the most enjoyable traditions of the religious persuasion of your choice, or secular practices of your choice, with respect for the religious/secular persuasions and/or traditions of others, or their choice not to practise religious or secular traditions at all . . .

...and a fiscally successful, personally fulfilling and medically uncomplicated recognition of the onset of the generally accepted calendar year 2004, but not without due respect for the calendars of choice of other cultures whose contributions to society have helped make America great (not to imply that the US of A is necessarily greater than any other country), and without regard to the race, creed, colour, age, physical ability, religious faith, choice of computer platform, educational attainment, union or non-union affiliation, or sexual preference of the wishee.

(By accepting this greeting, you are accepting these terms. This greeting is subject to clarification or withdrawal. It is freely transferable with no alteration to the original greeting. It implies no promise by the wisher to actually implement any of the wishes for her/himself or others, and is void where prohibited by law, and is revocable at the sole discretion of the wisher. This wish is warranted to perform as expected within the usual application of good tidings for a period of one year, or until the issuance of a subsequent holiday greeting, whichever comes first, and warranty is limited to replacement of this wish or issuance of a new wish at the sole discretion of the wisher.)

Bill Jamieson wrote an article in *The Scotsman* in December 2003 on the topic, "The state is trying to kill off Christmas". He wrote:

> People have long bemoaned the commercialisation of Christmas. But there is another, graver, threat to the spirit of this religious festival: a growing assertion by the state that Christmas would be better celebrated without Christianity at all. This year, the Scottish Parliament banned its officials from sending Christmas cards with a religious theme. Church officials in High Wycombe, meanwhile, were prevented from advertising a carol service in local libraries for fear it would offend non-Christians. Such are the sacrifices demanded by the high priests of social inclusion. The card that best captures the new manners is the one sent by the Culture Secretary, Tessa Jowell. It is a postmodern collage featuring ethnic tribal dancers, a television set, a train and the word "goal". Short of sending out an entirely blank card, Ms Jowell has absolutely got it: none of the images is Christian, or even seasonal. This is how the modern state would have us celebrate Christ's birth: with meaningless prattle as proxy for faith.

Until one feels the spirit of Christmas, there is no Christmas. All else is outward display – so much tinsel and decorations. For,

> *It isn't the holly, it isn't the snow,*
> *It isn't the tree nor the firelight's glow,*
> *It's the warmth that comes to the hearts of men*
> *When the Christmas spirit returns again.*

Most people gain around 5lbs over Christmas, having consumed 6,000 calories on Christmas Day alone.

On the **FIRST** day of Christmas this is what I ate: a scrumptious piece of chocolate Christmas cake.

On the **SECOND** day of Christmas this is what I ate: two mince pies and a scrumptious piece of chocolate Christmas cake.

On the **THIRD** day of Christmas this is what I ate: three sausage rolls, two mince pies and a scrumptious piece of chocolate Christmas cake.

On the **FOURTH** day of Christmas this is what I ate: four roasted spuds, three sausage rolls, two mince pies and a scrumptious piece of chocolate Christmas cake.

On the **FIFTH** day of Christmas this is what I ate: five Christmas puuuuuuuuds, four roasted spuds, three sausage rolls, two mince pies and a scrumptious piece of chocolate Christmas cake.

On the **SIXTH** day of Christmas this is what I ate: six balls of stuffing, five Christmas puuuuuuuuds, four roasted spuds, three sausage rolls, two mince pies and a scrumptious piece of chocolate Christmas cake.

On the **SEVENTH** day of Christmas this is what I ate: seven chipolatas, six balls of stuffing, five Christmas puuuuuuuuds, four roasted spuds, three sausage rolls, two mince pies and a scrumptious piece of chocolate Christmas cake.

On the **EIGHTH** day of Christmas this is what I ate: eight brandy butters, seven chipolatas, six balls of stuffing, five Christmas puuuuuuuuds, four roasted spuds, three sausage rolls, two mince pies and a scrumptious piece of chocolate Christmas cake.

On the **NINTH** day of Christmas this is what I ate: nine Brussels sprouts, eight brandy butters, seven chipolatas, six balls of stuffing, five Christmas puuuuuuuuds, four roasted spuds, three sausage rolls, two mince pies and a scrumptious piece of chocolate Christmas cake.

On the **TENTH** day of Christmas this is what I ate: ten cheesy crackers, nine Brussels sprouts, eight brandy butters, seven chipolatas, six balls of stuffing, five Christmas puuuuuuuuds, four roasted spuds, three sausage rolls, two mince pies and a scrumptious piece of chocolate Christmas cake.

On the **ELEVENTH** day of Christmas this is what I ate: eleven plates of turkey, ten cheesy crackers, nine Brussels sprouts, eight brandy butters, seven chipolatas, six balls of stuffing, five Christmas puuuuuuuuds, four roasted spuds, three sausage rolls, two mince pies and a scrumptious piece of chocolate Christmas cake.

On the **TWELFTH** day of Christmas this is what I ate: twelve chocolate Santas, eleven plates of turkey, ten cheesy crackers, nine Brussels sprouts, eight brandy butters, seven chipolatas, six balls of stuffing, five Christmas puuuuuuuuds, four roasted spuds, three sausage rolls, two mince pies and a scrumptious piece of chocolate Christmas cake.

On the THIRTEENTH day of Christmas....

BLEEAARRRR

It was Christmas time. The trip had gone reasonably well, but the traveller was ready to go back home.

The airport, on the other hand, had turned a tacky red and green, and loudspeakers blared annoying elevator renditions of cherished Christmas carols.

Being someone who took Christmas very seriously, and being slightly tired, the traveller was not in a particularly good mood. Going to check in his luggage (which, for some reason, had become one suitcase filled entirely with new clothes), he saw some hanging mistletoe. Not real mistletoe, but very cheap plastic with white paint on some of the rounder parts and green paint on some of the flatter and pointier parts; something that could be taken for mistletoe only in a very Picasso sort of way.

With a considerable degree of irritation and nowhere else to vent it, he said to the pretty young attendant, "Even if I were not married, I would not want to kiss you under such a ghastly mockery of mistletoe."

"Sir, look more closely at where the mistletoe is."

(pause)

"OK, I see that it's above the luggage scale, which is the place you'd have to step forward for a kiss."

"That's not why it's there."

(pause)

"OK, I give up. Why is it there?"

"It's there so you can kiss your luggage goodbye."

In Washington a TV reporter was working on an assignment called "The spirit of Christmas", so he called the British embassy and asked to speak to the British ambassador.

"Ambassador," the reporter said, "you have been very kind to us through the year and we would like to include you in a Christmas news segment we're going to run. Tell me, what would you like for Christmas?"

The ambassador replied, "I am very touched by your offer, but I must decline to accept any gift."

"Oh, please," said the reporter. "You really have been very helpful to us, so won't you please tell me what you would especially like for Christmas?"

Again the ambassador refused, but the reporter persisted and he finally gave in. "All right, then, if you insist. This Christmas I would like a jar of mint jelly."

Having forgotten about the conversation, the ambassador was surprised when, several weeks later, he turned on the evening news and heard the same reporter introducing a segment on "The spirit of Christmas":

> We recently interviewed three visiting ambassadors and asked them what they would like for Christmas. These three diplomats each gave revealing answers when they pondered what they would most like during this Christmas season of goodwill.
>
> The German ambassador said: "I would like to see a peaceful and prosperous year ahead for all citizens of the planet. May God bless us all."
>
> The Swiss ambassador said: "May the Spirit of Christmas last throughout the year. It is my dream that our world leaders will be guided towards a common goal of peaceful co-existence. This is my wish this Christmas season."
>
> And then we asked the British ambassador, who said, "I would like a jar of mint jelly."

A Sunday school teacher asked her class, "What was Jesus' mother's name?" One child answered, "Mary".

The teacher then asked, "Who knows what Jesus' father's name was?" A little kid said, "Verge".

Confused, the teacher asked, "Where did you get that from?"

The kid said, "Well, you know how they are always talking about 'Verge and Mary'."

Two young boys were spending the night at their grandparents' house, the week before Christmas. At bedtime, as the two boys knelt beside their beds to say their prayers, the younger one began praying at the top of his lungs: "I pray for a new bicycle! I pray for a new Nintendo! I pray for a new VCR!"

His older brother leaned over and nudged the younger boy and said, "Why are you shouting your prayers? God isn't deaf."

To which the little brother replied, "No, but Grandma is!"

'Twas the day after Christmas, and all through the house,
Every creature was hurtin', even the mouse.
The toys were all broken, their batteries dead;
Santa passed out, with some ice on his head.

Wrapping and ribbons just covered the floor,
While upstairs the family continued to snore.
And I in my T-shirt, new Reeboks and jeans,
I went into the kitchen and started to clean.

When out on the lawn there arose such a clatter,
I sprang from the sink to see what was the matter.
Away to the window I flew like a flash,
Tore open the curtains, and threw up the sash.

When what to my wondering eyes should appear,
But a little white truck, with an oversized mirror.
The driver was smiling, so lively and grand;
The patch on his jacket said "US Postman".

With a handful of bills, he grinned like a fox,
Then quickly he stuffed them into our mailbox.
Bill after bill, after bill, they still came,
Whistling and shouting he called them by name:

"It's Macy's, then Bloomies, now Penney's and Wal-Mart,
Here's Robinsons, Sears and Best Buy, and Target.
To the tip of your limit, every store, every mall,
Now charge away – charge away – charge away all!"

He whooped and he whistled as he finished his work,
He filled up the box, and then turned with a jerk.
He sprang to his truck and he drove down the road,
Driving much faster with just half a load.

Then I heard him exclaim with great holiday cheer,
"Enjoy what you bought... You'll be paying all year!"

CHURCH

A church decided to have four separate worship services each Sunday. There was one service for those people who were new to the faith, another for regular members who preferred the more traditional worship service, one for those who'd lost their faith and wanted to get it back, and a service for those who had had some unsuccessful experiences with other churches and had some complaints.

The four divisions were named: Finders, Keepers, Losers, Weepers.

"The church is the only co-operative society in the world that exists for the benefit of its non-members."
William Temple

CHURCHGOING

In one church, the pastor, apparently fed up with all the excuses given over the years as to why people don't go to church, included "Ten reasons why I never wash" in the Sunday bulletin:

1. I was forced to as a child.
2. People who wash are hypocrites – they think they are cleaner than everybody else.
3. There are so many different kinds of soap, I can't decide which one is best.
4. I used to wash, but I got bored and stopped.
5. I wash only on special occasions, like Christmas and Easter.
6. None of my friends wash.
7. I'll start washing when I get older and dirtier.
8. I can't spare the time.
9. The bathroom is never warm enough in winter or cool enough in summer.
10. People who make soap are only after your money.

François Fenelon was the court preacher for King Louis XIV of France in the 17th century. One Sunday, when the king and his attendants arrived at the chapel for the regular service, no one else was there but the preacher. King Louis demanded, "What does this mean?"

Fenelon replied, "I had published that you would not come to church today, in order that your Majesty might see who serves God in truth and who flatters the king."

COMMUNICATION

Dear Son,

The other day I went up to our local Christian bookstore and saw a "Honk if you love Jesus" bumper sticker. I was feeling particularly upbeat that day because I had just come from a thrilling worship celebration, followed by a thunderous prayer meeting. So I bought the sticker and put it on my bumper. Boy, I'm glad I did! What an uplifting experience followed!

I was stopped at a red light at a busy intersection, just lost in thought about the Lord and how good he is, and I didn't notice that the light had changed. It is a good thing someone else loved Jesus because if he hadn't honked, I'd never have noticed. I found that lots of people love Jesus! Why, while I was sitting there, the guy behind started honking like crazy and then he leaned out of his

...it most certainly is not a good luck sign, young man! I'll tell you exactly what it means....

window and screamed, "For the love of God! Go! Go! Go! Go!" What an exuberant cheerleader he was for Jesus!

Everyone started honking! I just leaned out my window and started waving and smiling at all those loving people. I even honked my horn a few times to share in the love!

There must have been a man from Florida back there because I heard him yelling something about a "sunny beach". I saw another guy waving in a funny way...with only his middle finger stuck in the air. Then I asked my teenage grandson in the back seat what it meant. He said it was probably a Hawaiian good luck sign or something. Well, I've never met anyone from Hawaii, so I leaned out the window and gave him the good luck sign back. My grandson burst out laughing...why, even he was enjoying this religious experience!

A couple of the people were so caught up in the joy of the moment that they got out of their cars and started walking towards me. I bet they wanted to pray or ask what church I attended.

This is when I noticed the light had changed. So, I waved and smiled at all my brothers and sisters, and drove on through the intersection. I noticed I was the only car that got through the intersection before the light changed again and I felt kind of sad that I had to leave them after all the love we shared.

So I slowed the car down, leaned out the window, and gave them all the Hawaiian good luck sign as I drove away. Praise the Lord for such wonderful folks!

Will write again soon,

Love, Mom

A minister with a large family of seven children moved to a new city. He and his wife didn't want to buy a home immediately. They wanted to rent a townhouse until they could get a feel for the area and choose a home where their kids would be in good schools and they could be conveniently located.

They found plenty of rental townhouses that were large enough, but the landlords always objected to having a family of nine occupy the place.

In frustration, one day the father asked the mother to take the four youngest children and go visit the local cemetery. She was puzzled by his request, but went along. He and the other three children headed off to investigate another townhouse they had found.

The place was perfect and the father told the landlord he would take it. Then came the usual question, "I see you have children. How many are there in the family?"

The minister gave out a deep sigh, then said, "Seven...but four are with their dear mother in the cemetery."

He got the townhouse.

MEMO   From: Headquarters   To: General Managers
Next Thursday at 10:30 Halley's Comet will appear over this area. This is an event which occurs only once every 75 years. Notify all directors and have them arrange for all employees to assemble on the company lawn and inform them of the occurrence of this phenomenon. If it rains, cancel the day's observation and assemble in the auditorium to see a film about the comet.

MEMO   From: General Manager   To: Managers
By order of the Executive Vice President, next Thursday at 10:30, Halley's Comet will appear over the company lawn. If it rains, cancel the day's work and report to the auditorium with all employees where we will show films: a phenomenal event which occurs every 75 years.

MEMO   From: Manager   To: All Department Chiefs
By order of the phenomenal Vice President, at 10:30 next Thursday, Halley's Comet will appear in the auditorium. In case of rain over the company lawn, the Executive Vice President will give another order, something which occurs only every 75 years.

MEMO   From: Department Chief   To: Section Chiefs
Next Thursday at 10:30 the Executive Vice President will appear in the auditorium with Halley's Comet, something which occurs every 75 years. If it rains, the Executive Vice President will cancel the comet and order us all out to our phenomenal company lawn.

MEMO   From: Section Chief   To: All
When it rains next Thursday at 10:30 over the company lawn, the phenomenal 75-year-old Executive Vice President will cancel all work and appear before all employees in the auditorium accompanied by Bill Haley and his Comets.

CONFESSION

"A psychologist asked various prisoners, 'Why are you here?' The answers were very revealing, though expected:
    'I was framed.'
    'They ganged up on me.'
    'It was a case of mistaken identity.'
    The psychologist wondered if one could possibly find a larger group of innocent people anywhere else but in prison!"

John Maxwell

CONFUSION

A do-it-yourself catalogue firm received the following letter from one of its customers:

I built a birdhouse according to your stupid plans, and not only is it much too big, it keeps blowing out of the tree.
Signed,
Unhappy.

The firm replied:

Dear Unhappy,
We're sorry about the mix-up. We accidentally sent you a sailboat blueprint. But if you think you are unhappy, you should read the letter from the guy who came in last in the yacht club regatta.

CONSCIENCE

There is no pillow so soft as a clear conscience.

Conscience is the inner voice that warns us someone may be looking.

An imperfect conscience needs a perfect Guide.

Conscience does not get its guidance from a Gallup poll.

"Most of us follow our conscience as we follow a wheelbarrow. We push it in front of us in the direction we want to go."
Billy Graham

COURAGE

"All our dreams can come true – if we have the courage to pursue them."
Walt Disney

"It is easy to be brave from a safe distance."
Aesop

"Courage is contagious. When a brave man takes a stand, the spines of others are stiffened."
Billy Graham

"I never thought much about the courage of the lion-tamer. Inside the cage he is at least safe from people."
George Bernard Shaw

"If God wanted us to be brave, why did he give us legs?"
Marvin Kitman

"He that will not sail till all dangers are over must never put to sea."
Thomas Fuller

"Valour grows by daring; fear by holding back."

Publius Syrus

"Courage is being scared to death...and saddling up anyway."
John Wayne

"Courage is the power to let go of the familiar."
Raymond Lindquist

"God grant me the courage not to give up what I think is right, even though I think it is hopeless."
Chester W Nimitz

"Courage is fear holding on a minute longer."
George S Patton

"One ought never to turn one's back on a threatened danger and try to run away from it. If you do that, you will double the danger. But if you meet it promptly and without flinching, you reduce the danger by half. Never run away from anything."
Winston Churchill

Courage **57**

CREATION

"On the return trip home, gazing through 240,000 miles of space toward the stars and the planet from which I had come, I suddenly experienced the universe as intelligent, loving, harmonious."

Edgar Mitchell, US astronaut

"We had the sky, up there, all speckled with stars, and we used to lay on our backs and look up at them, and discuss whether they was made, or only just happened".

Mark Twain, *Huckleberry Finn*

"I don't think you can be up here and look out the window as I did the first day and see the Earth from this vantage point, to look out at this kind of creation and not believe in God. To me, it's impossible – it just strengthens my faith."

John Glenn, broadcast from the *Discovery* space shuttle on 1 November 1998

"Two things continue to fill the mind with ever-increasing awe and admiration: the starry heavens above and the moral law within."

Immanuel Kant

"The earth reminded us of a Christmas tree ornament hanging in the blackness of space. As we got farther and farther away it diminished in size. Finally it shrank to the size of a marble, the most beautiful marble you can imagine. That beautiful, warm, living object looked so fragile, so delicate, that if you touched it with a finger it would crumble and fall apart. Seeing this has to change a man, has to make a man appreciate the creation of God and the love of God."

James Irwin, US astronaut

" 'I say!' murmured Horton, 'I've never heard tell
Of a small speck of dust
That is able to yell.
So you know what I think?
Why I think that there must
Be someone on top of
That small speck of dust!' "

Dr Seuss

"Once we see, however, that the probability of life originating at random is so utterly minuscule as to make it absurd, it becomes sensible to think that the favourable properties of physics on which life depends are in every respect deliberate... It is therefore almost inevitable that our own measure of intelligence must reflect...higher intelligences...even to the limit of God."
Sir Fred Hoyle, British mathematician, astronomer and cosmologist

*"**The human mind is not capable of grasping the universe. We are like a little child entering a huge library. The walls are covered to the ceilings with books in many different tongues. The child knows that someone must have written these books. It does not know who or how. It does not understand the languages in which they are written. But the child notes a definite plan in the arrangements of the books...a mysterious order which it does not comprehend but only dimly suspects.**"*
Albert Einstein

"The universe begins to look more like a great thought, than a great machine."
Sir James Jeans

"Remember that we can always look backward in time by looking out farther into space with our telescopes. The farther into space we look, the closer to the beginning we come."
Stephen Hawking

"The heavens speak of the Creator's glory and the sky proclaims God's handiwork."
Psalm 19:1

"I find it as difficult to understand a scientist who does not acknowledge the presence of a superior rationality behind the existence of the universe as it is to comprehend a theologian who would deny the advances of science."
Wernher von Braun

"Astronomy leads us to a unique event, a universe which was created out of nothing, one with the very delicate balance needed to provide exactly the conditions required to permit life, and one which has an underlying (one might say 'supernatural') plan."
Arno Penzias, Nobel Prize-winner in physics

"Every common biological organism is more intricately articulated, more astoundingly put together, than the most sublime literary composition... Despite all evasions, the ultimate agency of intelligence stares one in the face."
Frederick Ferre

"My theology, briefly, is that the universe was dictated but not signed."
Christopher Morley

"**A**fter close on two centuries of passionate struggles, neither science nor faith has succeeded in discrediting its adversary. On the contrary, it becomes obvious that neither can develop normally without the other. And the reason is simple: the same life animates both. Neither in its impetus nor its achievements can science go to its limits without becoming tinged with mysticism and charged with faith."

Pierre Teilhard de Chardin

"I find it quite improbable that such order came out of chaos. There has to be some organizing principle. God to me is a mystery but he is also the explanation for the miracle of existence, why there is something instead of nothing."

Alan Sandage, winner of the Crawford Prize in astronomy

"Why, if we evolved on this earth alone and have known no other, do we sense a kinship between the mountains of earth and the mountains of Mars, and find beauty in the stars?"

Timothy Ferris

"If we need an atheist for a debate, we go to the philosophy department. The physics department isn't much use."

Robert Griffiths, winner of the Heinemann Prize in mathematical physics

> "The physicists are getting things down to the nitty-gritty, they've really just about pared things down to the ultimate details, and the last thing they ever expected to happen is happening. God is showing through... They've been scraping away at physical reality all these centuries, and now the layer of the little left we don't understand is so fine, God's face is shining right out at us."
>
> **John Updike**

THE CROSS

Jesus did not come merely to make God's love possible, but to make God's love visible.

Many people use "duct tape" to fix everything... God used nails.

1 cross + 3 nails = 4 given

DEATH

You really only have two choices for the final curtain: burial or cremation.

    If you're cremated, you will be making an ash of yourself.

    If you're buried, as petroleum comes from fossilised bones, you will be making a fuel of yourself.

DESTINY

"I was conscious of a profound sense of relief. At last I had the authority to give directions over the whole scene. I felt as if I were walking with destiny and that all my past life had been but preparation for this hour and for this trial."

Winston Churchill, 10 May 1940, on becoming prime minister

"I refuse to believe the notion that man is flotsam and jetsam in the river of life, unable to respond to the eternal forever that confronts him."
Dr Martin Luther King, Jr

DIRECTION

A man hated his wife's cat and one day decided to get rid of it. He drove 20 blocks away from home and dropped the cat there. As he arrived home, the cat was already walking up the driveway.

The next day, he decided to drop the cat 40 blocks away but the same thing happened. He kept on increasing the number of blocks but the cat kept on coming home before him.

At last, he decided to drive a few miles away, turn right, then left, past the bridge, then right again and another right, and so on and so on, until he reached what he thought was the perfect spot, where he pushed the cat out of the door.

Hours later, the man called his wife at home and asked her, "Jen, is the cat there?"

"Yes, of course. Why do you ask?" answered the wife.

Frustrated, the man said, "Put him on the phone. I'm lost and I need directions."

DISCIPLINE

"Coleridge is the supreme tragedy of indiscipline. Never did so great a mind produce so little. He left Cambridge University to join the army; he left the army because he could not rub down a horse; he returned to Oxford and left without a degree. He began a paper called 'The Watchman', which lived for ten numbers then died. It has been said of him, 'He lost himself in visions of work to be done, that always remained to be done. Coleridge had every poetic gift but one – the gift of sustained and concentrated effort.' In his hand and in his mind he had all kinds of books as he himself said 'completed save the transcription. I am on the eve,' he said, 'of sending to the press two octavo volumes.' But the books were never composed outside Coleridge's mind, because he would not face the discipline of sitting down, to write out. No one ever reached any eminence, and no one, having reached it, ever maintained it, without discipline."

William Barclay

DREAMS

"Go confidently in the direction of your dreams. Live the life you have imagined."
Henry David Thoreau

"Throw off the bowlines. Sail away from the safe harbour. Catch the trade winds in your sails. Explore. Dream. Discover."
Mark Twain

"The world needs dreamers and the world needs doers. But above all, the world needs dreamers who do."
Sarah Ban Breathnach

"A dream is a wish your heart makes when you're fast asleep."

Cinderella

When your dreams turn to dust, vacuum!

"Nothing happens unless first a dream."

Carl Sanburg

"A person will sometimes devote all their life to the development of one part of their body – the wishbone."

Robert Frost

"If you can dream it, you can do it."

Walt Disney

"If you have built castles in the air, your work need not be lost; that is where they should be. Now put the foundations under them."

Henry David Thoreau

Every day is another opportunity to make your dreams come true.

"The future belongs to those who believe in the beauty of their dreams."

Eleanor Roosevelt

To make your dream come true you have to stay awake.

"Cherish your visions and your dreams as they are the children of your soul, the blueprints of your ultimate accomplishments."

Napoleon Hill

 "Hold fast to dreams for if dreams die
Life is a broken-winged bird that cannot fly.
Hold fast to dreams for when dreams go
Life is a barren field frozen with snow."

Langston Hughes

DRIVING

Kermit: "Fozzie, where did you learn to drive?"
Fozzie: "I took a correspondence course."

When my son was practising driving to pass his test, we would let him drive to church every Sunday. That way we were already praying before we arrived at church.

The other day my wife and I were discussing formal and informal prayer. I said, "I do some of my best praying while I'm driving." And my wife agreed by saying, "I, too, do my best praying while you're driving."

The road to success is not straight. There is a curve called Failure, a loop called Confusion, speed bumps called Friends, red lights called Enemies, caution lights called Family. You will have flats called Jobs.

But if you have a spare called Determination, an engine called Perseverance, insurance called Faith, a driver called Jesus, you will make it to a place called Success.

Have you ever noticed? Anybody going slower than you is an idiot, and anyone going faster than you is a maniac.

Any man who can drive safely while kissing a pretty girl is simply not giving the kiss the attention it deserves.

Albert Einstein

Two cars are waiting at a stoplight. The light turns green, but the man in the first car doesn't notice it. A woman in the car behind him watches the traffic pass around them. She begins pounding on her steering wheel and yelling at the man to move. He doesn't move.

The woman is going ballistic inside her car, ranting and raving at the man, pounding on her steering wheel and dashboard, and then the light turns yellow. She begins to blow the car horn, flips him off, and screams at him. The man, hearing the commotion, looks up, sees the yellow light and accelerates through the intersection just as the light turns red.

The woman is beside herself, screaming in frustration as she misses her chance to get through the intersection. As she is still in mid-rant she hears a tap on her window and looks up into the barrel of a gun held by a very serious-looking policeman.

The police officer tells her to shut off her car while keeping both hands in sight. She complies, speechless at what is happening. After she shuts off the engine, the police officer orders her to exit her car with her hands up. She gets out of the car and he orders her to turn and place her hands on her car. She turns, places her hands on the car roof and quickly is cuffed and hustled into the patrol car. She is too bewildered by the chain of events to ask any questions and is driven to the police station where she is fingerprinted, photographed, searched, booked and placed in a cell.

After a couple of hours, a police officer approaches the cell and opens the door for her. She is escorted back to the booking desk where the original officer is waiting with her personal effects.

He hands her the bag containing her things and says, "I'm really sorry for this mistake. But you see, I pulled up behind your car while you were blowing your horn, flipping that guy off, and shouting at the car in front of you, and then I noticed the "Choose life" licence-plate holder, the "What would Jesus do?" and "Follow me to Sunday School" bumper stickers, and the chrome-plated Christian fish emblem on the trunk, so naturally I assumed you had stolen the car."

The best safety device in a car is a rearview mirror with a policeman in it.

Never drive faster than your
guardian angel can fly.

If it moves so **SLOW**, why is it called rush hour?

Never lend your car to someone to whom you have given birth.

"Patience is something you admire in the driver behind you and scorn in the one ahead."

Mac McCleary

My kids drive me crazy. I drive them everywhere else.

"When a man opens a car door for his wife, it's either a new car or a new wife."

Prince Philip

It's time for a new car when you double the value of your car every time you fill the tank.

EASTER

Someone said to Joseph of Arimathea, "That was such a beautiful, costly, hand-hewn tomb. Why did you give it to someone else to be interred in?"

"Oh," said Joseph, "he only needed it for the weekend."

"Because of Easter, our coffins are nothing but canoes bearing us across the Jordan River to fairer worlds on High."
Herman Melville, *Moby Dick*

Because of Good Friday you can look back and not be afraid.
Because of Easter you can look ahead and not be afraid.
Because of Ascension Day you can look up and not be afraid.
Because of Pentecost you can look in and not be afraid.

ENTHUSIASM

"Enthusiasm and persistence can make an average person superior. Indifference and lethargy can make a superior person average."
William Ward

EXAMS

These are metaphors from actual high-school essays...

His thoughts tumbled in his head, making and breaking alliances like underpants in a tumble dryer.

Her vocabulary was as bad as, like, whatever.

The hailstones leaped from the pavement, just like maggots when you fry them in hot grease.

Long separated by cruel fate, the star-crossed lovers raced across the grassy field toward each other like two freight trains, one having left York at 6:36 pm travelling at 55 mph, the other from Peterborough at 4:19 pm at a speed of 35 mph.

The plan was simple, like my brother Phil. But unlike Phil, this plan just might work.

The young fighter had a hungry look, the kind you get from not eating for a while.

He was as lame as a duck. Not the metaphorical lame duck either, but a real duck that was actually lame. Maybe from stepping on a land mine or something.

She had a deep, throaty, genuine laugh, like that sound a dog makes just before it throws up.

He was deeply in love. When she spoke, he thought he heard bells, as if she were a dustcart reversing.

She grew on him like she was a colony of *E. coli* and he was room-temperature British beef.

It hurt the way your tongue hurts after you accidentally staple it to the wall.

EXERCISE

Grandma started walking for her health when she was 60. She's now 97 and we don't know where she is!

"Whenever I think about exercise, I lie down 'til the thought passes."
Robert Hutchins

I have to exercise early in the morning before my brain figures out what I am doing.

"I'm not into working out. My philosophy: No pain, no pain."
Carol Leifer

If you're going to try cross-country skiing, start with a small country.

Aerobics: a series of strenuous exercises which help convert fats, sugars, and starch into aches, pains and cramps.

"The best remedy for a short temper is a long walk."
Jacqueline Schiff

EXPERIENCE

The personnel director was interviewing a job applicant.

"Given that you have no experience whatsoever in this field, you're asking for an awfully high salary," she pointed out.

"I suppose so," replied the applicant. "But think how much harder the work's going to be if I don't know anything about it."

Experience is the best teacher but the tuition is costly!

Experience is what you get when you didn't get what you wanted.

"Education is when you read the fine print. Experience is what you get if you don't."
Pete Seeger

FAITH

"Faith does not operate in the realm of the possible. There is no glory for God in that which is humanly possible. Faith begins where man's power ends."

George Müller

"For the truly faithful, no miracle is necessary. For those who doubt, no miracle is sufficient."

Nancy Gibbs

"Faith is like radar that sees through the fog."

Corrie ten Boom

Things looked bleak for the children of George Müller's orphanage at Ashley Down in England. It was time for breakfast and there was no food.

A small girl whose father was a close friend of Müller was visiting in the home. Müller took her hand and said, "Come and see what our Father will do."

In the dining room, long tables were set with empty plates and empty mugs. Not only was there no food in the kitchen, but there was no money in the home's account. Müller prayed, "Dear Father, we thank Thee for what Thou art going to give us to eat."

Immediately, they heard a knock at the door. When they opened it, there stood the local baker.

"Mr Müller," he said, "I couldn't sleep last night. Somehow I felt you had no bread for breakfast, so I got up at two o'clock and baked fresh bread. Here it is."

Müller thanked him and gave praise to God. Soon, a second knock was heard. It was the milkman. His cart had broken down in front of the orphanage. He said he would like to give the children the milk so he could empty the cart and repair it.

"Faith is taking the first step even when you don't see the whole staircase."
Dr Martin Luther King, Jr

Faith is not faith until it's all you're holding on to.

Faith is the bird who sings while it is still dark.

Feed your faith and your doubts will starve to death.

He who loses money loses much;
He who loses a friend loses more;
He who loses faith loses all.

Sorrow looks back;
Worry looks around;
Faith looks up!

"Faith is not belief without proof, but trust without reservation."
D Elton Trueblood

"All I have seen teaches me to trust the Creator for all I have not seen."
Ralph Waldo Emerson

FIRE

A fire started on some grassland near a farm in Indiana. The fire department from the nearby town was called to put the fire out, but it proved to be more than the small town fire department could handle, so someone suggested that a rural volunteer fire department be called. Though there was doubt that they would be of any assistance, the call was made.

The volunteer fire department arrived in a dilapidated old fire truck. They drove straight towards the fire and stopped in the middle of the flames. The volunteer firemen jumped off the truck and frantically started spraying water in all directions. Soon they had snuffed out the centre of the fire, breaking the blaze into two easily controllable parts.

The farmer was so impressed with the volunteer fire department's work, and so grateful that his farm had been spared, that he presented the volunteer fire department with a cheque for $1,000.

A local news reporter asked the volunteer fire captain what the department planned to do with the funds. "That should be obvious," he responded. "The first thing we're gonna do is get the brakes fixed on that stupid fire truck."

FISHING

A man went out to fish on a frozen lake. He cut a hole in the ice, dropped his line in and sat for hours without so much as a nibble.

After a while, a boy came along and cut a hole nearby. He baited his line, dropped it in the hole, and within a few minutes caught a fish. He baited his line again, and within another few minutes he had another fish.

The man was incensed, so he went over to the boy and asked him his secret.

"Roo raf roo reep ra rums rrarm."

"What was that?" the man asked.

Again the boy replied, "Roo raf roo reep ra rums rrarm."

"Look, I can't understand a word you're saying."

The boy spat into his hand and said, "You have to keep the worms warm!"

A bad day of fishing is still better than a good day at the office!

Fisherman's prayer: Lord, help me to catch a fish so large that even I, in the telling of it, never need to lie.

People and fish are alike. They both get into trouble when they open their mouths.

"Three-fourths of the earth's surface is water, and one-fourth is land. It is quite clear that the good Lord intended us to spend triple the amount of time fishing as taking care of the lawn."
Chuck Clark

"The two best times to fish is when it's rainin' and when it ain't."
Patrick F McManus

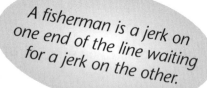
A fisherman is a jerk on one end of the line waiting for a jerk on the other.

Lord, help me see the day when I catch the one that got away!

Wanted: Good woman who can cook, sew, clean fish, has boat and motor. Send photo of boat and motor!

"There's no taking trout with dry breeches."
Miguel de Cervantes

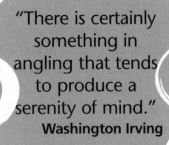
"There is certainly something in angling that tends to produce a serenity of mind."
Washington Irving

"If fishing is interfering with your business,
give up your business."

Alfred W Miller

"I am not against golf, since I cannot but suspect it keeps armies
of the unworthy from discovering trout."

Paul O'Neil

"Calling fly-fishing a hobby is like calling brain surgery a job."

Paul Schullery

***"Fishing is boring, unless you catch an actual fish,
and then it is disgusting."***

Dave Barry

My rod and my reel, they comfort me.

FOCUS

He who seeks one thing, and but one,
May hope to achieve it before life is done.
But he who seeks all things wherever he goes
Must reap around him in whatever he sows
A harvest of barren regret.

"I have only one purpose, the destruction of Hitler, and my life is much simplified thereby."

Winston Churchill

FORGIVENESS

"Forgiveness is God's command."
Martin Luther

"I can only say: however much we have been wronged, however justified our hatred, if we cherish it, it will poison us. Hatred is a devil to be cast out, and we must pray for the power to forgive, for it is in forgiving our enemies that we are healed."

Sheila Cassidy
(imprisoned by Pinochet)

"Human societies could not exist without forgiveness and the public acts of contrition and confession that make reconciliation possible."
Hannah Arendt, political philosopher

"Forgiveness is unlocking the door to set someone free and realizing you were the prisoner!"
Max Lucado

"He who cannot forgive breaks the bridge over which he himself must pass."
Thomas Fuller

"Once a woman has forgiven a man she must not reheat his sins for breakfast."
Marlene Dietrich

"Forgiveness is the fragrance the violet sheds on the heel that has crushed it."
Mark Twain

When you forgive, it takes you from the place of the victim to that of a victor.

"An ounce of apology is worth a pound of loneliness."
Joseph Joubert

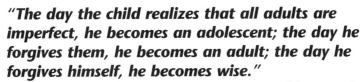

"The day the child realizes that all adults are imperfect, he becomes an adolescent; the day he forgives them, he becomes an adult; the day he forgives himself, he becomes wise."

Alden Nowlan

"Resentment is like taking poison and waiting for the other person to die."

Malachy McCourt

Holding a grudge is letting someone live rent free in your head.

FOUNDATIONS

The Leaning Tower of Pisa in Italy is one day going to fall. Scientists travel yearly to measure the building's slow descent. They report that the 179-foot tower moves about one-twentieth of an inch a year, and is now 17 feet out of plumb.

They further estimate that by the year 2007 the 810-year-old tower will have leaned too far and will collapse onto the nearby ristorante, where scientists now gather to discuss their findings.

Quite significantly, the word *pisa* means "marshy land", which gives some clue as to why the tower began to lean even before it was completed. Also, its foundation is only ten feet deep!

FRIENDSHIP

"A friend is the person who knows all about you and yet still likes you."

Elbert Hubbard

If you were going to die soon and had only one phone call you could make, who would you call and what would you say? And why are you waiting?

"You can make more friends in two months by becoming interested in other people than you can in two years by trying to get other people interested in you."

Dale Carnegie

Have you ever watched kids playing on a merry-go-round
Or listened to the rain lapping on the ground?
Ever followed a butterfly's erratic flight
Or gazed at the sun into the fading night?
Do you run through each day on the fly?
When you ask, "How are you?", do you hear the reply?

When the day is done, do you lie in your bed
With the next hundred chores running through your head?
Ever told your child, "We'll do it tomorrow"
And in your haste, not seen his sorrow?
Ever lost touch? Let a good friendship die?
Just call to say "Hi"!

When you worry and hurry through your day,
It is like an unopened gift...thrown away...
Life is not a race. Take it slower.
Hear the music before the song is over.

FUNERALS

An East End villain had a brother in the firm with him who died. He went to his local vicar and asked if he would hold a funeral service for his brother, and offered him £50,000 if he would say that his brother was a saint.

The vicar thought for a moment and then accepted the offer. But once he was back in his study and had time to reflect on his decision, he was full of regret, repentance and remorse before God. How could he now fulfill his word and yet hold on to his integrity as well as the money?

On the day of the funeral the vicar spoke of the deceased: "He was a rogue, a thief, a cheat and a liar," he said, "but compared with his brother he was a saint."

The secretary of a church, faced with the prospect of producing two funeral leaflets for the same day, complained to the minister of the parish about the extra work which this entailed. He, being dangerously computer-literate, advised her that, since the same form would be used for both services, she had only to employ the "search-and-replace" function to remove "Mary" (the first name of the departed) from the document and replace it with "Edna" for the second service.

All went well until the congregation arrived at the Creed: "…and in Jesus Christ his only Son our Lord, Who was conceived by the Holy Ghost, born of the Virgin Edna…"

GAFFES

The pastor of a church was famous for his pulpit gaffes. Once, he was speaking about the Ethiopian eunuch and Philip. He pointed out that the eunuch probably held high office, and expressed this by saying: "He had wealth, he had power, but he knew something was missing!" I nominate this for the understatement hall of fame.

GENERATIONS

According to today's regulators and bureaucrats, those of us who were kids in the 1950s, '60s, '70s and early '80s probably shouldn't have survived, because...

Our baby cots were covered with brightly coloured lead-based paint which was promptly chewed and licked.

We had no childproof lids on medicine bottles, or latches on doors or cabinets, and it was fine to play with pans.

When we rode our bikes, we wore no helmets, just flip-flops, and had fluorescent "clackers" on our wheels.

As children, we would ride in cars with no seat belts or air bags. Riding in the passenger seat was a treat.

We drank water from the garden hose and not from a bottle and it tasted the same.

We ate dripping sandwiches, bread-and-butter pudding and drank fizzy pop with sugar in it, but we were never overweight because we were always outside playing.

We shared one drink with four friends, from one bottle or can, and no one actually died!

We would spend hours building go-carts out of scraps and then went top speed down the hill, only to find out we'd forgotten the brakes.

After running into stinging nettles a few times, we learned to solve the problem.

We would leave home in the morning and play all day, as long as we were back before it got dark. No one was able to reach us all day and no one minded.

We did not have PlayStations or X-Boxes, no video games at all. No 99 channels on TV, no videotape movies, no surround sound, no mobile phones, no personal computers, no Internet chat rooms.

We had friends – we went outside and found them.

We played elastics and street rounders, and sometimes that ball really hurt.

We fell out of trees, got cut and broke bones and teeth, and there were no lawsuits. They were accidents. We learned not to do the same thing again.

We had fights, punched each other hard and got black and blue. We learned to get over it.

We walked to friends' homes.

We also, believe it or not, WALKED to school; we didn't rely on Mummy or Daddy to drive us to school, which was just round the corner.

We made up games with sticks and tennis balls and ate live stuff, and although we were told it would happen, we did not have very many eyes out, nor did the live stuff live inside us forever.

We rode bikes in packs of seven and wore our coats by only the hood.

Our actions were our own. Consequences were expected.

The idea of a parent bailing us out if we broke a law was unheard of. They actually sided with the law. Imagine that!

GIVING

The world's strongest man was touring with his show. For his finale he would take an orange, squeeze all the juice out of it and offer £1,000 to anyone in the audience who could get another drop of juice from it. Time after time, men came forward but, squeeze as they might, none could do it.

Then, one evening, a skinny old man came forward to meet the challenge. The crowd laughed at the idea that he could squeeze more juice than the strongest man. He calmly took the orange, put it between his palms – and to the crowd's amazement, out came a single drop of juice.

Handing over the £1,000, the stunned strongman couldn't resist asking the old man what he did for a living.

"I'm the treasurer for my local Anglican church."

GOD

God answers knee-mail.

"We regard God as an airman regards his parachute; it's there for emergencies but he hopes he'll never have to use it."
C S Lewis

H G Wells was never particularly religious, but after he had studied the history of the human race and had observed human life, he came to an interesting conclusion: "Religion is the first thing and the last thing, and until a man has found God and been found by God, he begins at no beginning, he works to no end. He may have his friendships, his partial loyalties, his scraps of honour. But all these things fall into place and life falls into place only with God."

When someone challenged Galileo to explain how God could be so powerful and yet care for every person, he replied:

"The sun, with all those planets revolving around it and dependent on it, can still ripen a bunch of grapes as if it had nothing else in the universe to do."

"One and God make a majority."
Frederick Douglass

"God loves each of us as if there were only one of us."
St Augustine

"I believe in God like I believe in the sunrise; not because I can see it but because I can see all that it touches."
C S Lewis

"I know God will not give me anything I can't handle. I just wish that he didn't trust me so much."
Mother Teresa

"God gave you a gift of 86,400 seconds today. Have you used one to say 'thank you?'"
William A Ward

"There are two kinds of people: those who say to God, 'Thy will be done,' and those to whom God says, 'All right, then, have it your way.'"
C S Lewis

"I have discovered that when the Almighty wants me to do or not do a particular thing, he has a way of letting me know it."
Abraham Lincoln

His mercies are new every morning, because our messes are new every day.

Peace on the outside comes from knowing God on the inside.

Until a person's hands are empty they cannot reach the hand of God.

God wants spiritual fruit, not religious nuts.

God brings people into deep waters not to drown them, but to cleanse them.

If you are not as close to God as you used to be, who moved?

God will never lead you where his grace cannot keep you.

Those who live in the Lord never see each other for the last time.

T.G.I.F. – Thank God I'm Forgiven!

The Bible is the only book where the author is always present whenever it is read.

Coincidence is when God chooses to remain anonymous.

God's Favourite department: Lost and Found.

A person whose Bible is falling apart usually isn't.

Download your worries. Get online with God.

"O God of Second Chances and New Beginnings, Here I am again."
Nancy Spiegelberg

He who kneels before God can stand before anyone.

"I believe that with the loss of God, man lost a kind of absolute and universal system of co-ordinates, to which he could always relate anything, chiefly himself. If God is not there, then we can no longer speak of meaning, of purpose, of accountability, of responsibility."
Vaclav Havel, former president of the Czech Republic

GOSSIP

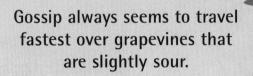

Gossip always seems to travel fastest over grapevines that are slightly sour.

Gossip is like an egg; when hatched it has wings.

If you are tempted to reveal
A tale to you someone has told about another,
Make it pass,
Before you speak,
Three gates of gold.
These narrow gates:
First, "Is it true?"
Then, "Is it needful?"
In your mind give truthful answer.
And the next is last and narrowest,
"Is it kind?"
And if to teach your lips at last
It passes through these gateways three,
Then you may tell the tale,
Nor fear what the result of speech may be.

One day a man saw at a distance his vicar hugging the wife of another church member. He was shocked. The first thing he did was tell other members of the church what he had seen, "just between the two of us".

That Sunday the vicar announced that one of the members of the church had suffered a terrible tragedy earlier in the week. It turned out that what the gossiping church member had seen was the vicar consoling this person's wife.

He was so ashamed that he went to his vicar and confessed what he had done, and asked for forgiveness, which he was granted.

The vicar asked the man to do him a favour. Because he felt so guilty, he jumped at the chance. So the vicar said to him,

"Take this feather pillow to the top of the hill in the centre of town, tear it open and release all the feathers to the wind, then come back to me when you have finished."

The church member obliged, convinced that he knew the lesson he was being taught. When he came back to the vicar, he told him that he understood the lesson, that gossip can spread quickly and easily.

The vicar said, "That is true, but for the most important part of the lesson: go and pick up every feather."

GRACE

"When a person works an eight-hour day and receives a fair day's pay for his time, that is a wage. When a person competes with an opponent and receives a trophy for his performance, that is a prize. When a person receives appropriate recognition for his long service or high achievements, that is an award. But when a person is not capable of earning a wage, can win no prize, and deserves no award – yet receives such a gift anyway – that is a good picture of God's unmerited favour. This is what we mean when we talk about the grace of God."

G W Knight

GRATITUDE

A young soldier was in his bunkhouse all alone one Sunday morning in the desert. It was quiet that day; the guns and the mortars, and the landmines, for some reason hadn't made a noise. The young soldier knew it was Sunday, the holiest day of the week. As he was sitting there, he got out an old deck of cards and laid them out across his bunk.

Just then an army sergeant came in and said, "Why aren't you with the rest of the platoon?"

The soldier replied, "I thought I would stay behind and spend some time with the Lord."

The sergeant said, "Looks like you're going to play cards."

The soldier said, "No, sir, you see, since we are not allowed to have Bibles or other spiritual books in this country, I've decided to talk to the Lord by studying this deck of cards."

The sergeant asked in disbelief, "How will you do that?"

"You see:

"The Ace reminds me that there is only one God.

"The Two represents the two parts of the Bible: Old and New Testaments.

"The Three represents the Father, the Son, and the Holy Spirit.

"The Four stands for the four apostles: Matthew, Mark, Luke and John.

"The Five is for the five bridesmaids that had enough oil in their lamps.

"The Six is for the six days it took God to create the heavens and earth.

"The Seven is for the day God rested after working the six days.

"The Eight is for the eighth day, the day the risen Jesus appeared to his disciples.

"The Nine is for the lepers that Jesus cleansed of leprosy but who didn't say 'thank you'.

"The Ten represents the ten commandments.

"The Jack is a reminder of Satan – an angel who rebelled and is now the knave of hell.

"The Queen stands for the Bride of Christ, the church.

"The King stands for Jesus, for he is the King of all kings.

"When I count the dots on all the cards, I come up with 365 total, one for every day of the year.

"There are a total of 52 cards in a deck; each is a week, the 52 weeks of the year.

"The four suits represent the four seasons: spring, summer, fall and winter, ordained by God.

"Each suit has thirteen cards; there are exactly thirteen weeks in a quarter.

"So when I want to talk to God, I just pull out this old deck of cards and they remind me of all that I have to be thankful for."

BEAT THAT—
THREE LEPERS

TWO LOUSEY PAIRS:
TESTAMENTS
AND COMMANDMENTS

YES! TWO BRIDES,
THREE TRINITIES!
FULL HOUSE!

PAIR OF SATANS
AND ONE GOD HIGH

It is gratitude that prompted an old man to visit an old broken pier on the eastern seacoast of Florida. Every Friday night, until his death in 1973, he would return, walking slowly and slightly stooped, with a large bucket of shrimp. The seagulls would flock to this old man, and he would feed them from his bucket.

Many years before, in October 1942, Captain Eddie Rickenbacker was on a mission in a B-17 to deliver an important message to General Douglas MacArthur in New Guinea. But there was an unexpected detour which would hurl Captain Eddie into the most harrowing adventure of his life.

Somewhere over the South Pacific the Flying Fortress became lost beyond the reach of radio. Fuel ran dangerously low, so the men ditched their plane in the ocean… For nearly a month Captain Eddie and his companions fought the water, and the weather, and the scorching sun. They spent many sleepless nights recoiling as giant sharks rammed their rafts. The largest raft was nine feet by five. The biggest shark…ten feet long.

But of all their enemies at sea, one proved most formidable: starvation. Eight days out, their rations were long gone or destroyed by the salt water. It would take a miracle to sustain them. And a miracle occurred.

In Captain Eddie's own words, "Cherry [the B-17 pilot, Captain William Cherry] read the service that afternoon, and we finished with a prayer for deliverance and a hymn of praise. There was some talk, but it tapered off in the oppressive heat. With my hat pulled down over my eyes to keep out some of the glare, I dozed off…

"Something landed on my head. I knew that it was a seagull. I don't know how I knew, I just knew. Everyone else knew too. No one said a word, but peering out from under my hat brim without moving my head, I could see the expression on their faces. They were staring at that gull. The gull meant food…if I could catch it."

And the rest, as they say, is history. Captain Eddie caught the gull. Its flesh was eaten. Its intestines were used for bait to catch fish. The survivors were sustained and their hopes renewed because a lone seagull, uncharacteristically hundreds of miles from land, offered itself as a sacrifice.

You know that Captain Eddie made it. And now you also know that he never forgot. Because every Friday evening, about sunset, on a lonely stretch along the eastern Florida seacoast, you could see an old man walking…white-haired, bushy-eyebrowed, slightly bent. His bucket filled with shrimp was to feed the gulls…to remember that one which, on a day long past, gave itself without a struggle…like manna in the wilderness.

HARDSHIP

 "In Italy for 30 years under the Borgias they had warfare, terror, murder and bloodshed, but they produced Michelangelo, Leonardo da Vinci, and the Renaissance. In Switzerland, they had brotherly love; they had 500 years of democracy and peace and what did they produce? The cuckoo clock."

Orson Welles

HEAVEN

A man arrives at the pearly gates. St Peter looks through his book and says, "Well, I see here that you weren't especially bad, but you weren't especially good either. If you can tell me one really good deed you've performed, I'll let you in."

The man replied, "Yeah. There was this one time when I was driving down the road when I saw this big group of bikers, about 30 of 'em, picking on this young woman. Well, I couldn't sit idly by. I grabbed a tyre lever out of the boot, walked right up to the leader of the gang, bonked him on the head with the tyre lever, then yelled at the rest of the bikers, 'Listen here, you bullies! You leave this poor defenceless woman alone! Get out of here before I teach you all a lesson!'"

"Wow!" St Peter says, clearly impressed. "When did this happen?"

"Oh, about five minutes ago."

The day finally arrives. Forrest Gump dies and goes to heaven. He walks up to the pearly gates and is met by St Peter himself. The good saint says, "Well, Forrest, we're glad to see you. We've heard a lot about you. I must let you know, however, that the place is filling up fast, so we've been giving an entrance examination to everyone.

"The test is short but you have to pass before you can get into heaven. You need to answer these three questions:

1. What days of the week begin with the letter "T"?
2. How many seconds are there in a year?
3. What is God's first name?

Forrest says, "Well, the first one – that's an easy one. There are two of them, Today and Tomorrow."

The saint's eyes open wide in surprise: "Forrest, that's not what I was thinking, but…I'll give you credit for that answer. How about the second question?"

"Now, that one's harder," says Forrest, "but I'll guess the answer to be 'twelve'."

Astounded, St Peter says, "Twelve? Twelve? Forrest, how could you come up with twelve seconds in a year?"

"Shucks, there's gotta be twelve," Forrest answers. "January 2nd, February 2nd, March 2nd, etc."

"Hold it," interrupts St Peter. "I see where you're going with this, and I'll have to give you credit for that one, too. Let's go on to the next and final question. Can you tell me God's first name?"

"Sure," Forrest replies. "It's Andy."

"Andy?" exclaims the exasperated and frustrated saint. "OK, I can understand how you came up with your answers to my first two questions, but just how in the world did you come up with the name of 'Andy' as the first name of God?"

"Oh," Forrest replies, "that was the easiest one of all: ANDY WALKS WITH ME, ANDY TALKS WITH ME, ANDY TELLS ME I AM HIS OWN."

St Peter opens the pearly gates and says, "Run, Forrest, run!"

The gains of heaven will more than compensate for the losses of earth.

After they had listened attentively to the morning lesson, the teacher smiled at her Sunday School class and exclaimed, "All right, class, all those who want to go to heaven, raise your hands."

Everybody in the class had a hand raised, except one boy. "Don't you want to go to heaven?" asked the teacher.

"I can't, ma'am," came the reply. "My mum wants me to come straight home after church and I can't go anywhere without her permission."

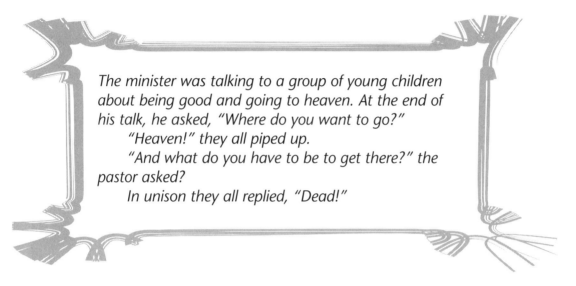

The minister was talking to a group of young children about being good and going to heaven. At the end of his talk, he asked, "Where do you want to go?"

"Heaven!" they all piped up.

"And what do you have to be to get there?" the pastor asked?

In unison they all replied, "Dead!"

HELPING

I was visiting a primary school to write a report on an incident of vandalism, when I was interrupted by a little girl who looked about six. She looked up and down at my uniform and asked, "Are you a policeman?"

"Yes, I am," I replied, and went back to my report.

"My mummy said if I ever needed help I should ask a policeman. Is that right?"

"Yes, it is," I told her.

"Well, then," she said, extending her foot towards me, "could you tie my shoelace, please?"

"Life's most persistent and urgent question is: What are you doing for others?"
Dr Martin Luther King, Jr

"Unless life is lived for others it is not worthwhile."

Mother Teresa

HOLIDAYS

The top seven signs that your vicar needs a vacation:

7. You caught him snoring during the service while he was leading the congregational prayer
6. The last ten sermons had the word "rest" in the title
5. The closing hymn for the last three weeks has been "I'll fly away"
4. At last weekend's service he showed up in a Hawaiian shirt and Bermuda shorts
3. Before the last board meeting, holiday brochures of exotic getaways were placed on each seat
2. The preacher's wife has posted a picture of him all over the neighbourhood with the caption: "Have you seen this man?"

And the number-one sign your preacher needs a vacation:

1. The theme of his Jonah sermon was – "A change of scenery does a person good!"

"Please go away" (sign on a travel agent's door)

The ark, the ship that carried a male and female of every living creature on earth, was the last cruise ship that was evenly matched.

HOPE

A rabbi asks his students, "How can we determine the hour of dawn, when the night ends and the day begins?"

One student suggests, "When, from a distance, you can distinguish between a dog and a sheep."

"No," the rabbi answers.

"Is it when you can distinguish between a fig tree and a grapevine?" asks a second student.

"No," the rabbi says.

"Please tell us the answer, then," say the students.

"It is," says the wise teacher, "when you have enough light to look human beings in the face and recognise them as your brothers and sisters. Until then the darkness is still with us."

 "Hope deferred makes the heart sick."
Proverbs 13:12

HOSPITALITY

"Nothing is more pleasant than the tie of host and guest."
Aeschylus,
fifth century BC

On Tuesday, 11 September 2001 a US passenger jet – Delta 15 – was flying over the north Atlantic when the Twin Towers came down. The plane was ordered to land at the nearest airport, so the crew headed for Newfoundland to Gander Airport.

Forty minutes later they landed to find 53 other airplanes on the ground from all over the world. The passengers were told that each and every plane was to be offloaded, one at a time. The following morning, at 11:00 am, it was their turn.

A flight attendant takes up the story:

A convoy of school buses showed up at the side of the airplane, the stairway was hooked up and the passengers were taken to the terminal for "processing". The crew were taken to the same terminal but were told to go to a different section, where we were processed through Immigration and Customs and then had to register with the Red Cross. After that we were isolated from our passengers and were taken in a caravan of vans to a very small hotel in the town of Gander. We had no idea where our passengers were going.

The town of Gander has a population of 10,400 people, and these folks now found themselves giving hospitality to 10,500 passengers and crew. Our 218 passengers ended up in a town called Lewisporte. There they were put in a high school. If any women wanted to be in a women-only facility, that was arranged. Families were kept together. All the elderly passengers were given no choice and were taken to private homes. A young pregnant lady was put up in a private home right across the street from a 24-hour Urgent Care facility. There were doctors on call and they had both male and female nurses available who stayed with the crowd for the duration. Phone calls and e-mails to the US and Europe were available for everyone once a day.

During the days, the passengers were given a choice of "excursion" trips. Some people went on boat cruises of the lakes and harbours. Some went to see the local forests. Local bakeries stayed open to make fresh bread for the guests. Food was prepared by all the residents and brought to the school for those who elected to stay put. Others were driven to the eatery of their choice and fed. They were given tokens to go to the local laundromat to wash their clothes, since their luggage was still on the aircraft. In other words, every single need was met for those unfortunate travellers.

When our passengers came on board, it was like they had been on a cruise. Everybody knew everybody else by name. They were swapping stories of their stay, impressing each other with who had the better time. It was mind-boggling. Our flight back to Atlanta looked like a party flight. We simply stayed out of their way. The passengers had totally bonded and they were calling each other by their first names, exchanging phone numbers, addresses, and e-mail addresses.

And then a strange thing happened. One of our business-class passengers approached me and asked if he could speak over the PA to his fellow passengers. We never allow that. But something told me to get out of his way. I said, "Of course".

The gentleman picked up the PA and reminded everyone about what they had just gone through in the last few days. He reminded them of the hospitality they had received at the hands of total strangers. He further stated that he would like to do something in return for the good folks of the town of Lewisporte. He said he was going to set up a trust fund under the name of "Delta 15". The purpose of the trust fund would be to provide a scholarship for high-school students of Lewisporte to help them go to college. He asked for donations of any amount from his fellow travellers.

When the paper with donations got back to us with the amounts, names, phone numbers and addresses, it totalled $14,500. The gentleman who started all this turned out to be a doctor from Virginia. He promised to match the donations and to start the administrative work on the scholarship. He also said that he would forward this proposal to Delta Corporate and ask them to donate as well.

Why all of this? Just because some people in faraway places were kind to some strangers, who happened to literally drop in among them.

There was a little old cleaning woman who went to the local church. When the invitation was given at the end of the service, she went forward, wanting to become a member. The pastor listened as she told him how she had accepted Jesus and wanted to be baptised and become a member of the church.

The pastor thought to himself, "Oh my, she's so unkempt, even smells a little, and her fingernails aren't clean. She picks up garbage, cleans toilets – what would the members think of her?" He told her that she needed to go home and pray about it and then decide.

The following week, here she came again. She told the pastor that she had prayed about it and still wanted to be baptised. "I've passed this church for so long. It's so beautiful, and I truly want to become a member."

Again the pastor told her to go home and pray some more.

A few weeks later, while out eating at the restaurant, the pastor saw the little old lady. He didn't want her to think he was ignoring her, so he approached her and said, "I haven't seen you for a while. Is everything all right?"

"Oh, yes," she said. "I talked with Jesus, and he told me not to worry about becoming a member of your church."

"He did?" said the pastor.

"Oh, yes," she replied. "He said even he hasn't been able to get into your church yet, and he's been trying for years."

HOWLERS

"Smoking kills. If you're killed, you've lost a very important part of your life."

Brooke Shields, during an interview to become spokesperson for a federal anti-smoking campaign

"Sure, it's going to kill a lot of people, but they may be dying of something else anyway."

Othal Brand, member of a Texas pesticide review board, on chlordane

"You've got to be very careful if you don't know where you're going because you might not get there."
Yogi Berra

"You could be a winner! No purchase necessary. Details inside" (label spotted on a bag of Fritos Corn Chips)

Ten things said by Murray Walker…

1. "I make no apologies for their absence – I'm sorry they're not here."
2. "So, with half the race gone there's half the race to go."
3. "Now excuse me while I interrupt myself."
4. "Either the car is stationary or it's on the move."
5. "Patrick Tambay's hopes, which were nil before, are absolutely zero now."
6. "I imagine that the conditions in those cars today are totally unimaginable."
7. "I wonder if he's in the relaxed state of mind that he is in."
8. "The atmosphere is so tense you could cut it with a cricket stump."
9. "The lead car is absolutely unique – except for the one behind it, which is identical."
10. "Do my eyes deceive me or is Senna's Lotus sounding a bit rough?"

"The streets are safe in Philadelphia. It's only the people who make them unsafe."
Frank Rizzo, ex-police chief and mayor of Philadelphia

"After finding no qualified candidates for the position of principal, the school board is extremely pleased to announce the appointment of David Steele to the post."
Philip Streifer, superintendent of schools, Barrington, Rhode Island

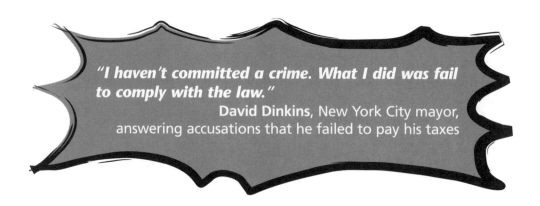

"I haven't committed a crime. What I did was fail to comply with the law."
David Dinkins, New York City mayor, answering accusations that he failed to pay his taxes

"The police are not here to create disorder. They're here to preserve disorder."
Richard Daley, former Chicago mayor, during the infamous 1968 Democratic convention

"Traditionally, most of Australia's imports come from overseas."
Keppel Enderbery, former Australian cabinet minister

Correctly English in 100 Days
(title of an East Asian book for English beginners)

"We don't like their sound, and guitar music is on the way out."
Decca Recording Company, rejecting the Beatles, 1962

Things are more like they are now than they ever were before.
Dwight D Eisenhower, former US president

"Today is Father's Day, so everyone out there: Happy Birthday!"
Ralph Kiner, announcer for the New York Mets

"Hijackers should be given a rapid trial...
with due process of law at the airport, then hanged."
Edward Davis, police chief of Los Angeles in 1973

"I've never had major knee surgery on any other part of my body."
Winston Bennett, University of Kentucky basketball forward

"I intend to open this country up to democracy, and
anyone who is against that, I will jail, I will crush."
General Joao Baptista Figueiredo, elected president of Brazil in 1979

"Patient failed to fulfil his wellness potential."
(doctor's note on the chart of a patient who died)

"I didn't accept it. I received it."
Richard Allen, National Security Advisor to President Reagan,
explaining the $1,000 in cash and two watches he was given
by two Japanese journalists after he helped arrange
a private interview for them with First Lady Nancy Reagan

HUMILITY

The story is told of the famous boxer Muhammad Ali, who was flying one time to an engagement. The aircraft ran into severe turbulence and was soon being shaken violently. The passengers were all instructed to fasten their seatbelts straightaway. Everyone complied except Ali.

Noticing this, a stewardess approached him and asked him to fasten his belt. Ali replied, "Superman don't need no seat belt." The stewardess took one look at him and retorted, "Superman don't need no airplane either!"

HUMOUR

"A keen sense of humour helps us to overlook the unbecoming, understand the unconventional, tolerate the unpleasant, overcome the unexpected, and outlast the unbearable."

Billy Graham

Everyone laughs in the same language.

"A laugh is a smile that bursts."

Mary H Waldrip

"Laughter is an instant vacation."

Milton Berle

"We are all here for a spell; get all the good laughs you can."

Will Rogers

"The human race has only one really effective weapon and that is laughter."
Mark Twain

Every survival kit should include a sense of humour.

IDEAS

"Great spirits have always encountered opposition from mediocre minds."
Albert Einstein

"The best ideas are common property."
Seneca

"A mind once stretched by a new idea never regains its original dimension."
Oliver Wendell Holmes

"A new idea is delicate. It can be killed by a sneer or a yawn; it can be stabbed to death by a quip and worried to death by a frown on the right man's brow."
Charles Brower

"Don't worry about people stealing your ideas. If your ideas are any good, you'll have to ram them down people's throats."
Howard Aiken,
IBM engineer

"No great discovery was ever made without a bold guess."
Sir Isaac Newton

"If you want to get across an idea, wrap it up in a person."
Ralph Bunche

IMPOSSIBILITIES

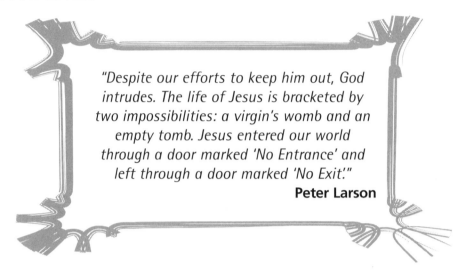

"Despite our efforts to keep him out, God intrudes. The life of Jesus is bracketed by two impossibilities: a virgin's womb and an empty tomb. Jesus entered our world through a door marked 'No Entrance' and left through a door marked 'No Exit.'"

Peter Larson

INDUSTRY

Some years ago a former American astronaut took over as head of a major airline, determined to make the airline's service the best in the industry. One day, as the new president walked through a particular department, he saw an employee resting his feet on a desk while the telephone on the desk rang incessantly. "Aren't you going to answer that phone?" the boss demanded.

"This isn't my department," answered the employee nonchalantly, apparently not recognising his new boss. "I work in maintenance."

"Not any more you don't!" snapped the president.

John Wesley travelled 250,000 miles on horseback, averaging 20 miles a day for 40 years; preached 4,000 sermons; produced 400 books; knew ten languages. At 83 he was annoyed that he could not write more than fifteen hours a day without hurting his eyes, and at 86 he was ashamed he could not preach more than twice a day. He complained in his diary that there was an increasing tendency to lie in bed until 5:30 in the morning.

INTELLIGENCE

"I do not feel obliged to believe that the same God who endowed us with sense, reason and intellect, has intended us to forgo their use."
Galileo

Light travels faster than sound. This is why some people appear bright until you hear them speak.

JOY

"The gloom of the world is but a shadow. Behind it, yet within reach, is joy. There is a radiance and glory in the darkness, could we but see, and to see, we have only to look. I beseech you to look."

Fra Giovanni

"Grief can take care of itself, but to get the full value of a joy you must have somebody to divide it with."

Mark Twain

"It is not how much we have, but how much we enjoy, that makes happiness."

Charles Spurgeon

"Joy does not simply happen to us. We have to choose joy and keep choosing it every day. It is a choice based on the knowledge that we belong to God and have found in God our refuge and our safety and that nothing, not even death, can take God away from us. Joy is the experience of knowing that you are unconditionally loved and that nothing – sickness, failure, emotional distress, oppression, war, or even death – can take that love away."

Henri Nouwen

"I don't really care how I am remembered as long as I bring happiness and joy to people."
Eddie Albert

"Joy is very infectious; therefore, be always full of joy."
Mother Teresa

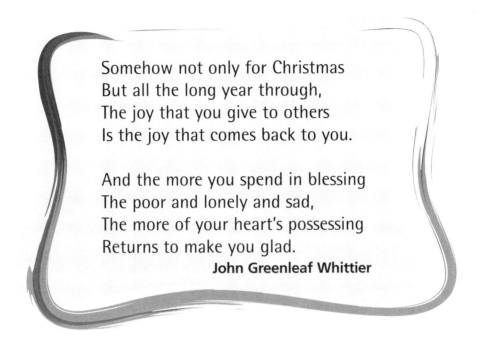

Somehow not only for Christmas
But all the long year through,
The joy that you give to others
Is the joy that comes back to you.

And the more you spend in blessing
The poor and lonely and sad,
The more of your heart's possessing
Returns to make you glad.

John Greenleaf Whittier

JUSTICE

Supreme Court Justice Horace Gray once informed a man who had appeared before him in a lower court and had escaped conviction on a technicality, "I know that you are guilty and you know it, and I wish you to remember that one day you will stand before a better and wiser Judge, and that there you will be dealt with according to justice and not according to law."

Surprised while burgling a house in Antwerp, Belgium, a thief fled out the back door, clambered over a nine-foot wall, dropped down the other side, and found himself in the city prison.

"All virtue is summed up in dealing justly."
Aristotle, *Nicomachean Ethics*

"I have always found that mercy bears richer fruits than strict justice."
Abraham Lincoln

"You mortals, the Lord has told you what is good.
This is what the Lord requires from you:
to do what is right,
to love mercy,
and to live humbly with your God."

Micah 6:8

"Almighty God, grant us grace fearlessly to contend against evil, and to make no peace with oppression; and, that we may reverently use our freedom, help us to employ it in the maintenance of justice among people and nations."

The Book of Common Prayer

"There may be times
when we are powerless to
prevent injustice, but there
must never be a time
when we fail to protest."
Elie Wiesel

KINDNESS

"A person who is nice to you, but rude to the waiter, is not a nice person."
Dave Barry

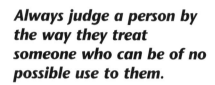

The best way to knock the chip off another person's shoulder is to pat him on the back!

"The best way to cheer yourself up is to try to cheer somebody else up."
Mark Twain

"That best portion of a good man's life: his little, nameless, unremembered acts of kindness and of love."
William Wordsworth

Always judge a person by the way they treat someone who can be of no possible use to them.

"Dare to reach out your hand into the darkness, to pull another hand into the light."
Norman B Rice

"We can do no great things, only small things with great love."
Mother Teresa

"It is difficult to give away kindness. It keeps coming back to you."
Cort Flint

"Do good and care not to whom."
Italian proverb

"Kindness is in our power, even when fondness is not."

Samuel Johnson

"Kindness is a language which the deaf can hear and the blind can read."

Mark Twain

"When a person is down in the world, an ounce of help is better than a pound of preaching."

Buliver

"You cannot do a kindness too soon, for you never know how soon it will be too late."

Ralph Waldo Emerson

"How far that little candle throws his beams! So shines a good deed in a weary world."
William Shakespeare

"The fragrance always stays in the hand that gives the rose."
Hadia Bejar

"Non-violence is the answer to the crucial political and moral questions of our time: the need for man to overcome oppression and violence without resorting to oppression and violence. Man must evolve for all human conflict a method which rejects revenge, aggression and retaliation. The foundation of such a method is love."
Dr Martin Luther King, Jr, Nobel Prize acceptance speech, Stockholm, Sweden, 11 December 1964

KISSING

At the end of their first date, a young man takes his favourite girl home. Emboldened by the night, he decides to try for that important first kiss. With an air of confidence, he leans with his hand against the wall and, smiling, he says to her, "Darling, how 'bout a goodnight kiss?"

Horrified, she replies, "Are you mad? My parents will see us!"

"Oh, come on! Who's gonna see us at this hour?"

"No, please. Can you imagine if we get caught?"

"Oh, come on, there's nobody around, they're all sleeping!"

"No way. It's just too risky!"

"Oh, please, please, I like you so much!!"

"No, no, and no. I like you too, but I just can't!"

"Oh yes you can. Please?"

"NO, no. I just can't."

"Pleeeeease…?"

Just then, the porch light goes on, and the girl's sister shows up in her pyjamas, hair dishevelled, and says in a sleepy voice:

"Dad says to go ahead and give him a kiss. Or I can do it. Or if need be, he'll come down himself and do it. But for goodness' sake tell him to take his hand off the intercom button!"

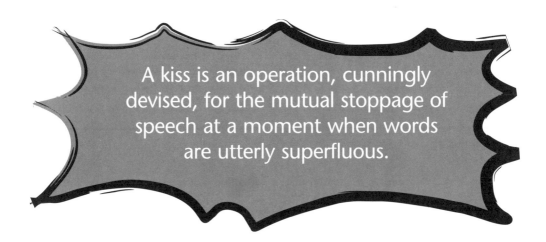

A kiss is an operation, cunningly devised, for the mutual stoppage of speech at a moment when words are utterly superfluous.

LAWSUITS

The Stella Awards are named after 81-year-old Stella Liebeck, who spilled coffee on herself and successfully sued McDonald's. That case inspired the "Stella Awards" for the most frivolous successful lawsuits in the United States.

The following were candidates:

1. Kathleen Robertson was awarded $780,000 by a jury of her peers after breaking her ankle tripping over a toddler who was running inside a furniture store. The owners of the store were understandably surprised at the verdict, considering the misbehaving little toddler was Ms Robertson's son!

2. Nineteen-year-old Carl Truman won $74,000 and medical expenses when his neighbour ran over his hand with a Honda Accord. Mr Truman apparently didn't notice there was someone at the wheel of the car when he was trying to steal his neighbour's hubcaps.

3. Terrence Dickson was leaving a house he had just finished robbing by way of the garage. He was not able to get the garage door to go up since the automatic door-opener was malfunctioning. He couldn't re-enter the house because the door connecting the house and garage had locked when he pulled it shut. The family was on vacation, and Mr Dickson found himself locked in the garage for eight days. He subsisted on a case of Pepsi he found, and a large bag of dry dog food. He sued the homeowner's insurance, claiming the situation caused him undue mental anguish. The jury agreed, to the tune of $500,000.

4. Jerry Williams was awarded $14,500 and medical expenses after being bitten on the buttocks by his next-door neighbour's beagle. The beagle was on a chain in its owner's fenced yard. The award was less than sought because the jury felt the dog might have been just a little provoked at the time by Mr Williams, who was shooting it repeatedly with a pellet gun.

5. A restaurant was ordered to pay Amber Carson $113,500 after she slipped on a soft drink and broke her coccyx. The beverage was on the floor because Ms Carson had thrown it at her boyfriend 30 seconds earlier during an argument.

6. Kara Walton successfully sued the owner of a nightclub when she fell from the bathroom window to the floor and knocked out her two front teeth. This occurred while Ms Walton was trying to sneak through the window in the ladies' room to avoid paying the $3.50 cover charge. She was awarded $12,000 and dental expenses.

7. This year's favourite could easily be Mr Merv Grazinski. Mr Grazinski purchased a brand new 32-foot Winnebago motor home. On his first trip home, having driven onto the freeway, he set the cruise control at 70 mph and calmly left the driver's seat to go into the back and make himself a cup of coffee. Not surprisingly, the vehicle left the freeway, crashed and overturned.

Mr Grazinski sued Winnebago for not advising him in the owner's manual that he couldn't actually do this. The jury awarded him $1,750,000, plus a new motor home. The company actually changed their manuals on the basis of this suit, just in case there were any other complete morons buying their recreation vehicles.

"If for all practical purposes we believe that this life is our best shot at happiness, if this is as good as it gets, we will live as desperate, demanding and eventually despairing men and women. We will place on this world a burden that it was never intended to bear. We will try to find a way to get back into the Garden and when that fails, as it always does, our hearts fail as well."

John Eldridge, *The Sacred Romance*

The secret of life is not to do what you like but to like what you do.

"Life is like an onion; you peel it off one layer at a time, and sometimes you weep."

Carl Sandburg

 "The true meaning of life is to plant trees under whose shade you do not expect to sit."

Nelson Henderson

LONELINESS

"I've never found a companion as companionable as solitude."
Henry David Thoreau

"With some people, solitariness is an escape not from others but from themselves. For they see in the eyes of others only a reflection of themselves."
Eric Hoffer

" 'Don't you want to join us?' I was recently asked by an acquaintance when he ran across me alone after midnight in a coffeehouse that was already almost deserted. 'No, I don't,' I said."
Franz Kafka

"Pray that your loneliness may spur you into finding something to live for, great enough to die for."
Dag Hammarskjöld

"What should young people do with their lives today? Many things, obviously. But the most daring thing is to create stable communities in which the terrible disease of loneliness can be cured."
Kurt Vonnegut

"There's nothing terribly wrong with feeling lost, so long as that feeling precedes some plan on your part to actually do something about it. Too often a person grows complacent with their disillusionment, perpetually wearing their 'discomfort' like a favourite shirt."
Jhonen Vasquez

"If you are alone you belong entirely to yourself... If you are accompanied by even one companion you belong only half to yourself, or even less, in proportion to the thoughtlessness of his conduct; and if you have more than one companion you will fall more deeply into the same plight."
Leonardo da Vinci

"There is absolutely no point in sitting around and feeling sorry for yourself. The great power you have is to let go... Focus on what you have, not that which has been mean or unkindly removed."

Minnie Driver

"The body is a house of many windows: there we all sit, showing ourselves and crying on the passers-by to come and love us."

Robert Louis Stevenson

"Better be alone than in bad company."

Thomas Fuller

"The whole conviction of my life now rests upon the belief that loneliness, far from being a rare and curious phenomenon, peculiar to myself and to a few other solitary men, is the central and inevitable fact of human existence."

Thomas Wolfe, *God's Lonely Men*

"One may have a blazing hearth in one's soul, and yet no one ever comes to sit by it."

Vincent van Gogh

"I never said, 'I want to be alone.' I only said, 'I want to be left alone.' There is all the difference."

Greta Garbo

"Our language has wisely sensed the two sides of being alone. It has created the word 'loneliness' to express the pain of being alone. And it has created the word 'solitude' to express the glory of being alone."

Paul Tillich

"No one would choose a friendless existence on condition of having all the other things in the world."

Aristotle

"To dare to live alone is the rarest courage; since there are many who had rather meet their bitterest enemy in the field, than their own hearts in their closet."

Charles Caleb Colton

"**W**hen Christ said: 'I was hungry and you fed me,' he didn't mean only the hunger for bread and for food; he also meant the hunger to be loved. Jesus himself experienced this loneliness. He came amongst his own and his own received him not, and it hurt him then and it has kept on hurting him. The same hunger, the same loneliness, the same having no one to be accepted by and to be loved and wanted by. Every human being in that case resembles Christ in his loneliness; and that is the hardest part, that's real hunger."

Mother Teresa

MANAGEMENT

The Americans and the Japanese decided to engage in a competitive boat race. Both teams practised hard and long to reach their peak performance. On the big day they felt ready.

The Japanese won by a mile. Afterward, the American team was discouraged by the loss. Morale sagged. Corporate management decided that the reason for the crushing defeat had to be found, so a consulting firm was hired to investigate the problem and recommend corrective action. The consultant's finding: the Japanese team had eight people rowing and one person steering; the American team had one person rowing and eight people steering.

After a year of study and millions spent analysing the problem, the consultant firm concluded that too many people were steering and not enough were rowing on the American team.

So, as race day neared again the following year, the American team's management structure was completely reorganised. The new structure: four steering managers, three area steering managers and a new performance review system for the person rowing the boat to provide work incentive.

That year, the Japanese won by two miles. Humiliated, the American corporation laid off the rower for poor performance and gave the managers a bonus for discovering the problem...

"I believe that managing is like holding a dove in your hand. If you hold it too tightly you will kill it, but if you hold it too loosely, you will lose it."

Tommy Lasorda

Several cannibals were recently hired by a big corporation. "You are all part of our team now," said the human resources representative during the welcome brief. "You get all the usual benefits and you can go to the cafeteria for something to eat, but please don't eat any other employees." The cannibals promised not to.

Four weeks later their boss remarked, "You're all working very hard and I'm really pleased with you. However, one of our secretaries has disappeared. Do any of you know what happened to her?" The cannibals all shook their heads: "No".

After the boss had left, the leader of the cannibals said to the others, "Which one of you idiots ate the secretary?" A hand was raised hesitantly, to which the leader of the cannibals continued, "You fool! For four weeks we've been eating managers and no one noticed anything, but nooooo, you had to go and eat a secretary!"

MARRIAGE

To keep a fire burning brightly there's one easy rule; keep the logs together, near enough to keep warm and far enough apart for breathing room. Good fire, good marriage. Same rule.

Communicating frequently and intimately is the best prescription for a successful marriage.

"A good marriage is the union of two forgivers."

Ruth Graham

The bonds of marriage aren't worth much unless the interest is kept up.

A man and a woman, who have never met before, find themselves assigned to the same sleeping room on a transcontinental train.

Though initially embarrassed and uneasy over sharing a room, the two are tired and fall asleep quickly – he in the upper bunk and she in the lower.

At 2:00 am, he leans over and gently wakes the woman, saying, "Ma'am, I'm sorry to bother you, but would you be willing to reach into the closet to get me a second blanket? I'm awfully cold."

"I have a better idea," she replies. "Just for tonight, let's pretend that we're married."

"Wow! That's a great idea!" he exclaims.

"Good," she replies. "Get your own blanket."

"Six ways to learn everything you ever need to know about a man before you decide to marry him: 1. Watch him drive in heavy traffic. 2. Play tennis with him. 3. Listen to him talk to his mother when he doesn't know you're listening. 4. See how he treats those who serve him (waiters, maids). 5. Notice what he's willing to spend his money to buy. 6. Look at his friends. And if you still can't make up your mind, then look at his shoes. A man who keeps his shoes in good repair generally tends to the rest of his life too."

Lois Wyse

Matrimony: the high sea for which no compass has yet been invented.

"By all means marry! If you get a good wife, you'll be happy. If you get a bad one, you'll become a philosopher."
Socrates

Courtship is like looking at the beautiful photos in a seed catalogue. Marriage is what actually comes up in your garden.

Just think, if it weren't for marriage, men would go through life thinking they had no faults at all.

D uring their wedding in December 2000, Madonna and Guy Ritchie were given an unusual gift by the Reverend Susan Brown, the Scottish minister who presided over the ceremony at the Church of Scotland's cathedral in Dornoch, Scotland. The gift? A twin-pack of toilet paper.

"There are two rolls together," she later explained, "just like the couple. And the toilet paper is soft, gentle, long and strong – which is what I hope their marriage will be."

The seven secrets of a successful marriage
by Susan Quilliam

Secret 1: Successful Married Couples get their deal straight
Successful couples talk deeply before the wedding about their expectations of each other, and if there's serious disagreement – for example, he wants kids, she doesn't – they think seriously about whether to marry.

Secret 2: Successful Married Couples keep their individuality
Successful couples know that, however much love there is, marriage can bring this trapped feeling. They encourage each other not to be always "us", to take "me" time, to have "me" hobbies and even "me" friends.

Secret 3: Successful Married Couples keep each other centre stage
Successful couples always keep each other centre stage. They are interested in their partner's opinions. They take their partner seriously. They refer to their spouse in glowing terms when talking to other people.

Secret 4: Successful Married Couples learn to resolve conflicts
Successful couples keep communicating, whatever the bad feeling between them. They negotiate differences and disagreements so that they both end up getting a fair deal.

Secret 5: Successful Married Couples keep the passion alive
Successful couples stay affectionate. If there's a sexual drought, they ride it out by flirting, touching, hugging, kissing and being romantic.

Secret 6: Successful Married Couples grow with each other
Successful couples anticipate shifts and ride with them. Rather than demanding they both stay the same forever, they welcome the natural developments of personality and partnership that happen with time.

Secret 7: Successful Married Couples keep working at it
Successful couples take rain checks and keep having regular "where are we at" conversations to make sure that they're both happy with the way things are going.

Dear Tech Support,
Last year I upgraded from Boyfriend 5.0 to Husband 1.0 and noticed a distinct slowdown in overall system performance – particularly in the flower and jewellery applications, which operated flawlessly under Boyfriend 5.0.

In addition, Husband 1.0 uninstalled many other valuable programs, such as Romance 9.5 and Personal Attention 6.5, and then installed undesirable programs such as AFL 2.003, NFL 5.00, NBA 3.00 and Golf Clubs 4.1.

Conversation 8.0 no longer runs and Housecleaning 2.6 simply crashes the system.

I've tried running Nagging 5.3 to fix these problems but to no avail. What can I do?

Signed,
Desperate

Dear Desperate,
First keep in mind that Boyfriend 5.0 is an entertainment package while Husband 1.0 is an operating system.

Please enter the command: http:/I thought you loved me.htm and try to download Tears 6.2. Don't forget to install Guilt 3.0 update.

If that application works as designed, Husband 1.0 should then automatically run application Flowers 3.5 and Jewellery 2.0. But remember, overuse of this program can cause Husband to default to Grumpy Silence 2.5, Happy Hour 7.0 or Beer 6.1. Beer 6.1 is a very bad program that will download the Snoring Loudly Beta.

Whatever you do, DO NOT install Mother-In-Law 1.0 (it runs a virus in the background that will eventually seize control of all your system resources).

Also, do not attempt to re-install Boyfriend 5.0 program. This is an unsupported application and will crash Husband 1.0.

In summary, Husband 1.0 is a great program but it does have limited memory and cannot learn new applications quickly. You might consider buying additional software to improve memory and performance. We recommend Hot Food 3.0 and Lingerie 7.7.

Good luck,
Tech Support

MEMORY

The conductor Sir Thomas Beecham was attending a prestigious reception, and was in conversation with someone he recognised but whose name he could not recall. He began the conversation, desperate to find a clue to the person's identity. "So are you well?"

"Yes, thank you."

"And the family?"

"Yes, they are fine."

"And your husband, is he well?"

"Yes, very well, thank you."

"And is he still in the same line of business?"

"Yes, he's still king."

MEN AND WOMEN

There was a perfect man who met a perfect woman. After a perfect courtship, they had a perfect wedding. Their life together was, of course, perfect.

One snowy, stormy Christmas Eve, this perfect couple was driving their perfect car along a winding road, when they noticed someone at the side of the roadside in distress. Being the perfect couple, they stopped to help. There stood Santa Claus with a huge bundle of toys.

Not wanting to disappoint any children on the eve of Christmas, the perfect couple loaded Santa and his toys into their vehicle. Soon they were driving along delivering the toys.

Unfortunately, the driving conditions deteriorated and the perfect couple and Santa Claus had an accident. Only one of them survived the accident. Who was the survivor?

The perfect woman. She's the only one that really existed in the first place. Everyone knows there is no Santa Claus and there is no such thing as a perfect man...

We always hear the "rules" from the female side. Now here are the rules from the male side. These are our rules!

Learn to work the toilet seat. You're a big girl. If it's up, put it down. We need it up; you need it down. You don't hear us complaining about you leaving it down.

Weekend = sport. It's like the full moon or the changing of the tides. Let it be.

Shopping is not a sport. And no, we are never going to think of it that way.

Crying is blackmail.

Ask for what you want. Let us be clear on this one: subtle hints do not work! Strong hints do not work! Obvious hints do not work! Just say it!

"Yes" and "No" are perfectly good answers to almost every question!

Come to us with a problem only if you want help solving it. That's what we do. Sympathy is what your girlfriends are for.

A headache that lasts for 17 months is a problem. See a doctor.

Anything said six months ago is inadmissible in an argument. In fact, all comments become null and void after seven days.

If you think you're fat you probably are. Don't ask us.

If something we said can be interpreted two ways, and one way makes you sad and angry, we meant the other one.

You can either ask us to do something or tell us how you want it done. Not both. If you already know best how to do it, just do it yourself.

Whenever possible, please say what you want to say during commercials.

Christopher Columbus did not need directions and neither do we.

All men see in only 16 colours, like Windows default settings. Peach, for example, is a fruit, not a colour. Pumpkin is also a fruit. We have no idea what mauve is.

If it itches, it will be scratched. We do that.

If we ask you what is wrong and you say, "Nothing", we will act like nothing's wrong. We know you are lying, but it's not worth the hassle.

If you ask a question you don't want the answer to, expect an answer you don't want to hear.

When we have to go somewhere, absolutely anything you wear will be fine... Really.

Don't ask us what we're thinking about, unless you are prepared to discuss such topics as the offside rule, refereeing decisions, or off-roading.

You have enough clothes.

You have too many shoes.

I am in shape. Round is a shape.

Thank you for reading this. Yes, I know, I have to sleep on the couch tonight, but did you know, men really don't mind – it's like camping.

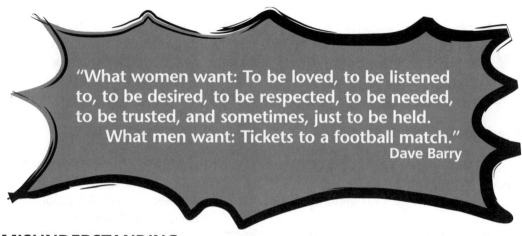

"What women want: To be loved, to be listened to, to be desired, to be respected, to be needed, to be trusted, and sometimes, just to be held. What men want: Tickets to a football match."
Dave Barry

MISUNDERSTANDING

There was a woman who spent some months serving God in Kenya. On her final visit to a remote township she attended a medical clinic. As the Maasai women there began to sing together, she found herself deeply moved by their beautiful harmonies. She wanted to always remember this moment and try to share it with friends when she arrived home.

With tears flowing down her cheeks, she turned to her friend and asked, "Can you please tell me the translation of the words to this song?"

Her friend looked at her and solemnly replied, "If you boil the water, you won't get dysentery."

MONEY

About the time we make ends meet, somebody moves the ends.

Budget: a method for going broke methodically.

A person is rich according to what he is, not according to what he has!

I am having an out-of-money experience.

One in five Britons suffer from financial phobia, a psychological condition which prevents them sorting out their personal finances.

According to research by Egg, the online bank, and a senior lecturer at Cambridge University, half the population show some symptoms of the syndrome.

Symptoms include feeling anxious, guilty, bored or out of control when managing their money, and this can lead to them not opening bank statements or checking account balances, or avoiding thinking about their money altogether.

The report estimates that up to nine million people suffer from the psychological and physiological condition.

Dr Brendan Burchell, of the Faculty of Social and Political Sciences at Cambridge University, says: "Financialphobes can be intelligent people who are high achievers in most areas of their lives – they are not irresponsible, feckless or spendthrifts.

"They have become entwined in this psychological syndrome which makes it very difficult for them to deal efficiently with their personal finances."

According to the research, 54% of sufferers feel apprehension when they have to deal with money matters, while 38% show complete lack of interest in their finances. People with the syndrome also suffer physical effects, with 45% claiming the prospect of having to deal with their finances sends their heart racing; 12% say they feel physically ill, 11% feel dizzy, and 15% become immobilised.

The condition is found among all classes and age groups, and its onset usually coincides with some form of financial upset, such as being mis-sold a financial product. Other causes putting off dealing with money matters can be frustration about the time and effort needed to make decisions, and a lack of confidence when confronted with complex financial information.

The highest levels of financial phobia are found among younger age groups, with 30% of 16- to 24-year-olds suffering from the condition and 26% of 25- to 34-year-olds. Women are also more likely to suffer from the condition than men.

The research was based on telephone interviews with 300 people in July and August, a focus-group discussion with five people and interviews with ten people in August, and a telephone survey of 1,000 people in September.

My yearnings exceed my earnings.

Money talks; mine keeps saying goodbye.

To feel rich, count the things you have that money can't buy.

"People are living longer than ever before, a phenomenon undoubtedly made necessary by the 30-year mortgage."
Doug Larson

Cashtration (n.) The act of buying a house, which renders the subject financially impotent for an indefinite period.

MOTHERS

Prayer of a mother

I gave you life, but cannot live it for you.
I can teach you things, but I cannot make you learn.
I can give you directions, but I cannot be there to lead you.
I can allow you freedom, but I cannot account for it.
I can take you to church, but I cannot make you believe.
I can teach you right from wrong, but I cannot always decide for you.
I can buy you beautiful clothes, but I cannot make you beautiful inside.
I can offer you advice, but I cannot accept it for you.
I can give you love, but I cannot force it upon you.
I can teach you to share, but I cannot make you unselfish.
I can teach you respect, but I cannot force you to show honour.
I can advise you about friends, but cannot choose them for you.
I can advise you about sex, but I cannot keep you pure.
I can tell you the facts of life, but I can't build your reputation.
I can tell you about drink, but I can't say "no" for you.
I can warn you about drugs, but I can't prevent you from using them.
I can tell you about lofty goals, but I can't achieve them for you.
I can teach you about kindness, but I can't force you to be gracious.
I can warn you about sins, but I cannot make you moral.
I can love you as a child, but I cannot place you in God's family.
I can pray for you, but I cannot make you walk with God.
I can teach you about Jesus, but I cannot make Jesus your Lord.
I can tell you how to live, but I cannot give you eternal life.

"Sweater, n.: garment worn by child when its mother is feeling chilly."

Ambrose Bierce

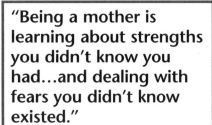

"Mother love is the fuel that enables a normal human being to do the impossible."

Marion C Garretty

"It is the mother who can cure her child's tears."

African proverb

Most mothers hate four-letter words, especially: cook, wash, iron and dust!

"Being a mother is learning about strengths you didn't know you had…and dealing with fears you didn't know existed."

Linda Wooten

"An ounce of mother is worth a pound of clergy."

Spanish proverb

A mother holds her children's hands for a while; their hearts forever.

"Mother – that was the bank where we deposited all our hurts and worries."

T Dewitt Talmage

A mother is someone with whom you may not see eye to eye, but is someone who will always walk with you arm in arm.

MOVIES

Movie-rating system explained:

G: Nobody gets the girl
PG: The good guy gets the girl
R: The bad guy gets the girl
X: Everybody gets the girl

N

NATURE

Never miss a rainbow or a sunset because you're looking down.

The earth laughs in flowers.

"People from a planet without flowers would think we must be mad with joy the whole time to have such things about us."
Iris Murdoch

"Everybody needs beauty, places to play in where nature may heal and cheer and give strength to the body and soul alike."
John Muir

"I go to nature to be soothed and healed, and to have my senses put in order."

John Burroughs

Nature is the art of God.

Spring is nature's way of saying, "Let's party!"

"The bluebird carries the sky on his back."
Henry David Thoreau

"The world is mud-luscious and puddle-wonderful."
E E Cummings

NEIGHBOURS

Chance made us neighbours. Hearts made us friends.

"To have a good neighbour is to find something precious."
Chinese proverb

A good neighbour is a found treasure!

Noah opens up the ark and lets all the animals out, telling them to "Go forth and multiply". He's closing the great doors of the ark when he notices that there are two snakes sitting in a dark corner.

So he says to them, "Didn't you hear me? You can go now. Go forth and multiply."

"We can't," said the snakes. "We're adders."

And so Noah goes up to God and says, "These snakes won't go forth and multiply as you've directed." And God says, "Don't worry, Noah. Find some trees, saw them into logs and create a platform sitting upon four legs. Then put the snakes on the platform."

"But how will that help the snakes?" asks Noah.

"Silly man, "replies God, "everyone knows even adders can multiply using a log table!"

The Lord spoke to Noah and said, "In six months I am going to make it rain until the whole world is covered with water and all the evil things are destroyed. But I want to save a few good people and two of every living thing on the planet. I am ordering you to build an ark." And, in a flash of lightning, he delivered the specifications for the ark.

"OK," Noah said, trembling with fear and fumbling with the blueprints, "I'm your man."

Six months passed, the sky began to cloud up, and the rain began to fall in torrents. The Lord looked down and saw Noah sitting in his yard, weeping, and there was no ark.

"Noah!" shouted the Lord, "where is my ark?" A lightning bolt crashed into the ground right beside Noah.

"Lord, please forgive me!" begged Noah. "I did my best, but there were some big problems. First, I had to get a building permit for the ark's construction, but your plans did not meet their code. So, I had to hire an engineer to redo the plans, only to get into a long argument with him about whether to include a sprinkler system.

"My neighbours objected, claiming that I was violating zoning ordinances by building the ark in my front yard, so I had to get a variance from the city planning board.

"Then, I had a big problem getting enough wood for the ark, because there was a ban on cutting trees to save the spotted owl. I tried to convince the environmentalists and the US Fish and Wildlife Service that I needed the wood to save the owls, but they wouldn't let me catch them, so no owls.

"Next, I started gathering up the animals but got sued by an animal rights group that objected to me taking along only two of each kind.

"Just when the suit got dismissed, the EPA notified me that I couldn't complete the ark without filling out an environmental impact statement on your 'proposed' flood. They didn't take kindly to the idea that they had no jurisdiction over the Supreme Being.

"Then, the Corps of Engineers wanted a map of the proposed flood plan. I sent them a globe.

"Right now, I'm still trying to resolve a complaint with the Equal Opportunities Commission over how many minorities I'm supposed to hire.

"The IRS has seized all my assets, claiming that I'm trying to leave the country, and I just got a notice from the state that I owe some kind of use tax.

Really, I don't think I can finish the ark in less than five years."

With that, the sky cleared, the sun began to shine, and a rainbow arched across the sky. Noah looked up and smiled. "You mean you're not going to destroy the world?"

"No," said the Lord. "The government already has."

LOOK - THEY'LL BE A LOT MORE ENDANGERED IF YOU DON'T LET ME TAKE THEM !

OBJECTIONS

 "Nothing will ever be attempted if all possible objections must be first overcome."

Samuel Johnson

OBSTACLES

Liu Chi Kung, who was placed second to Van Cliburn in the 1948 Tchaikovsky competition, was imprisoned a year later during the Cultural Revolution in China. During the entire seven years he was held, he was denied the use of a piano. Soon after his release, however, he was back on tour. Critics wrote in astonishment that his musicianship was better than ever. "How did you do this?" a critic asked. "You had no chance to practise for seven years."

"I did practise," Liu replied, "every day. I rehearsed every piece I have ever played, note by note, in my mind."

How To Maintain A Healthy Level Of Insanity In The Workplace

1. Page yourself over the intercom. Don't disguise your voice.
2. Find out where your boss shops and buy exactly the same clothes. Wear each outfit one day after your boss does. This is especially effective if your boss is of a different gender from you.
3. Make up nicknames for all your co-workers and refer to them only by these names. "That's a good point, Sparky." "I'm sorry, but I'm going to have to disagree with you there, Cha-cha."
4. Send e-mail to the rest of the company telling them exactly what you're doing. For example: "If anyone needs me, I'll be in the bathroom."
5. Hi-Lite your shoes. Tell people that you haven't lost them as much since you did this.
6. While sitting at your desk, soak your fingers in Palmolive liquid. Call everyone Madge.
7. Hang mosquito netting around your cubicle. When you emerge to get coffee or a printout or whatever, slap yourself randomly the whole way.
8. Place a chair facing a printer. Sit there all day and tell people you're waiting for your document.
9. Every time someone asks you to do something – anything – ask him or her if they want fries with that.
10. Send e-mail back and forth to yourself, engaging yourself in an intellectual debate. Forward the correspondence to a co-worker and ask her to settle the disagreement.
11. Encourage your colleagues to join you in a little synchronised chair-dancing.
12. Put your bin on your desk. Label it "IN".
13. Feign an unnatural and hysterical fear of staplers.
14. Send e-mail messages saying there's free pizza or doughnuts or cake in the lunchroom. When people drift back to work complaining that they found none, lean back, pat your stomach and say, "Oh, you've got to be faster than that."
15. Put decaf in the coffee-maker for three weeks. Once everyone has withdrawn from caffeine addiction, switch to espresso.

OLD AGE

"On Winston Churchill's 75th birthday, a photographer said, "I hope, sir, that I will shoot your picture on your hundredth birthday."
Churchill answered, "I don't see why not, young man. You look reasonably fit and healthy."

In one of Bruce Catton's final books, *Waiting for the Morning Train*, he captured this sense of passage as only he could: "Early youth is exactly like old age: it is a time of waiting for a big trip to an unknown destination. The chief difference is that youth waits for the morning limited and age waits for the night train."

A minister wished to meet after the service with a couple he was going to marry. Unfortunately, he couldn't remember their names, so he announced from the pulpit: "Will those wishing to be united in holy matrimony please come forward after the service."

Following the service, thirteen old spinsters came to the front!

Sometimes when I feel like I'm getting older I'm reminded of the little boy who was talking to his grandfather. The little boy said, "Grandpa, I heard you say that all the people who were alive when the flood came were killed, except for Noah and his family, because of their sin. Is that right?"

And the grandfather said, "That's right, son."

The little boy replied, "Well, if that's true, then how did you and grandma make it through?"

OPPORTUNITY

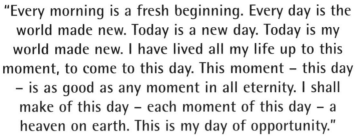

"Every morning is a fresh beginning. Every day is the world made new. Today is a new day. Today is my world made new. I have lived all my life up to this moment, to come to this day. This moment – this day – is as good as any moment in all eternity. I shall make of this day – each moment of this day – a heaven on earth. This is my day of opportunity."

Dan Custer

"You cannot afford to wait for perfect conditions. Goal-setting is often a matter of balancing timing against available resources. Opportunities are easily lost while waiting for perfect conditions."

Gary Ryan Blair

OPTIMISM

"Even if I knew that tomorrow the world would go to pieces, I would still plant my apple tree."
Dr Martin Luther King, Jr

"Grey skies are just clouds passing over."
Duke Ellington

"An optimist is the human personification of spring."
Susan J Bissonette

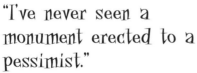
"I've never seen a monument erected to a pessimist."

Paul Harvey

ORGANISATION

A German soldier was wounded. He was ordered to go to the military hospital for treatment. When he arrived at the large and imposing building, he saw two doors, one marked, "For the slightly wounded", and the other, "For the seriously wounded".

He entered through the first door and found himself going down a long hall. At the end of it were two more doors, one marked, "For officers", and the other, "For non-officers". He entered through the latter and found himself going down another long hall. At the end of it were two more doors, one marked, "For party members" and the other, "For non-party members". He took the second door, and when he opened it he found himself out on the street.

When the soldier returned home, his mother asked him, "How did you get along at the hospital?"

"Well, Mother," he replied, "to tell the truth, the people there didn't do anything for me, but you ought to see the tremendous organisation they have!"

John Seamands

"Good order is the foundation of all things."
Edmund Burke, *Reflections on the Revolution in France*

"One person's mess is merely another person's filing system."
Margo Kaufman

"Begin at the beginning," the King said gravely, "and go till you come to the end; then stop."
Lewis Carroll

ORIGINALITY

"Your manuscript is both good and original, but the part that is good is not original, and the part that is original is not good."
Samuel Johnson

PARENTHOOD

"Don't worry that children never listen to you; worry that they are always watching you."

Robert Fulghum

"You will always be your child's favourite toy."
Vicki Lansky

"If you want your children to improve, let them overhear the nice things you say about them to others."

Haim Ginott

"Human beings are the only creatures on earth that allow their children to come back home."

Bill Cosby

"I didn't make the same mistakes my parents made when they raised me. I was too busy making new ones."

Bruce Lansky

"Children are a great comfort in your old age – and they help you reach it faster, too."

Lionel Kauffman

"What a child doesn't receive he can seldom later give."

P D James

"The child supplies the power, but the parents have to do the steering."

Benjamin Spock

"To bring up a child in the way he should go, travel that way yourself once in a while."

Josh Billings

Be kind to your kids; they pick your nursing home.

The quickest way for a parent to get a child's attention is to sit down and look comfortable.

*There are two things we should give our children:
one is roots, the other is wings.*

To be in your children's memories tomorrow, you have to be in their lives today.

You can't scare me – I have kids!

In the eyes of a child, love is spelled T-I-M-E.

Your children need your presence more than your presents.

Summer vacation is the time when parents realise that teachers are grossly underpaid.

Parents: a peculiar group who first try to get their children to walk and talk, and then try to get them to sit down and shut up.

PATIENCE

Patience is counting down without blast-off.

If God brings you to it, he will bring you through it.

"Patience is a bitter plant that produces sweet fruit."
Charles Swindoll

Patience is the ability to put up with people you'd like to put down.

 God grant me patience... NOW!

PEACEMAKERS

Since 3600 BC, the world has known only 292 years of peace!

During this period there have been 14,351 wars, large and small, in which 3.64 billion people have been killed.

The value of the property destroyed is equal to a gold belt around the world 97.2 miles wide and 33 feet thick.

Since 650 BC, there have also been 1,656 arms races, only 16 of which have not ended in war. The remainder ended in the economic collapse of the countries involved.

Telemachus was a monk who lived in the fourth century. He felt God saying to him, "Go to Rome", while he was in a cloistered monastery. He put his possessions in a sack and set out for Rome.

When he arrived in the city, people were thronging in the streets. He asked what all the excitement was about and was told that this was the day that the gladiators would be fighting and killing each other in the coliseum; this was the day of the games, the circus. He thought to himself, "Four centuries after Christ – and they are still killing each other, for enjoyment?"

Telemachus ran to the coliseum and heard the gladiators saying, "Hail to Caesar! We die for Caesar!" and he thought, "This isn't right." He jumped over the railing and went out into the middle of the arena, got between two gladiators, held up his hands and said, "In the name of Christ, forbear."

The crowd protested and began to shout, "Run him through! Run him through!" A gladiator came over and hit Telemachus in the stomach with the back of his sword. It sent him sprawling in the sand. He got up and ran back and again said, "In the name of Christ, forbear."

The crowd continued to chant, "Run him through!" One gladiator came over and plunged his sword through the little monk's stomach. He fell into the sand, which began to turn crimson with his blood. One last time he gasped out, "In the name of Christ, forbear."

A hush came over the 80,000 people in the coliseum. Soon a man stood and left, then another and then more, and within minutes all 80,000 had emptied out of the arena. It was the last known gladiatorial contest in the history of Rome.

> "God blesses those who work for peace, for they will be called the children of God."
> **Matthew 5:9**

PERSEVERANCE

Nineteenth-century inventor Gail Borden was obsessed with the idea of condensing food. His first effort, a condensed "meat biscuit", failed miserably. But an ocean voyage gave birth to a better idea.

Borden was concerned about the sickly condition of the children on board. Cows on the ship were too seasick to produce healthy milk, and four children died from drinking contaminated milk. Borden was determined to condense milk so that it would be safe and easily transported. After many tries, he devised a vacuum process that removed water from milk.

Conditions during the Civil War made the canned milk a success, and Borden made a fortune. His epitaph, inscribed on a tomb the shape of a milk can, was, "I tried and failed; I tried again and again, and succeeded."

"The person...who looks for quick results in the seed-planting of well-doing will be disappointed. If I want potatoes for dinner tomorrow, it will do me little good to go out and plant potatoes in my garden tonight.

There are long stretches of darkness and invisibility and silence that separate planting and reaping. During the stretches of waiting there is cultivating and weeding and nurturing and planting still other seeds."

Eugene Petersen

"Genius is 2% inspiration and 98% perspiration" (Thomas Edison). Edison worked 18-hour days and practised Herculean patience. Once he recognised the value of an idea, Edison stayed with the process until he discovered its secret. His alkaline storage battery became a reality after 10,000 (sic) failed experiments!

Thomas Edison's first teacher described him as "addled", and his father almost convinced him he was a "dunce".

Winston Churchill seemed so dull as a youth that his father thought he might be incapable of earning a living in England.

G K Chesterton, the English writer, could not read until he was eight. One of his teachers told him, "If we could open your head we should not find any brain but only a lump of white fat."

Albert Einstein's parents feared their child was dull, and he performed so badly in all high-school courses except mathematics that a teacher asked him to drop out.

Don't be discouraged. It's often the last key in the bunch that opens the lock.

"He who limps is still walking."

Stanislaw J Lec

"It's not that I'm so smart; it's just that I stay with problems longer."

Albert Einstein

"That which we obtain too easily, we esteem too lightly."

Thomas Paine

 IBM, General Electric and RCA all rejected the Xerox machine. Parker Brothers turned down Trivial Pursuit. The creators of Life Savers sold the company for $2,900. Don't give up!

PERSPECTIVE

Heavenly Father, help us to remember that the "jerk" who cut us off in traffic last night is a single mother who worked nine hours that day and is rushing home to cook dinner, help with homework, do the laundry and spend a few precious moments with her children.

Help us to remember that the pierced, tattooed, disinterested young man who can't make change correctly is a worried 19-year-old college student, balancing his apprehension over final exams with his fear of not getting his student loans for next term.

Remind us, Lord, that the scary-looking homeless man, begging for money in the same spot every day (who really ought to get a job!), is a slave to addictions that we can only imagine in our worst nightmares.

Help us to remember that the old couple walking annoyingly slowly through the store aisles and blocking our shopping progress are savouring this moment, knowing that, based on the biopsy report she got back last week, this will be the last year that they go shopping together.

Heavenly Father, remind us each day that, of all the gifts you give us, the greatest gift is love. It is not enough to share that love with those we hold dear. Open our hearts not just to those who are close to us, but to all humanity. Let us be slow to judge and quick to forgive and show patience, empathy and love.

PIGS

Mr Smith decided to branch out into pig-breeding, and so he went and bought 20 pigs. To his dismay he discovered that they were all sows, so he phoned his friend Mr Jones who had some prize boars, and arranged to bring his sows over to mate.

"How will I know if it has worked?" asked Mr Smith when he went round.

"Look out your window tomorrow morning," replied Mr Jones, "and if your pigs are grazing, then you're in business."

The next morning Mr Smith looked out, but his pigs were in the sty as usual. So he called Mr Jones again, and asked if he could bring them round again.

"Certainly," replied Mr Jones, so Mr Smith loaded the pigs in the lorry, took them round to Mr Jones', and let them mingle with his boars as before.

The next morning, he looked out of the window, and the pigs were still in the sty. Rather fed up, he arranged to take them around to Mr Jones' for a third time. He loaded them into his lorry, drove them round, let them mingle, loaded them up again and drove home.

The next morning he could not face looking out of the window in case he was disappointed. So he asked his wife to look instead. "Are the pigs in the sty or are they grazing?" he asked.

"Neither," said his wife. "Nineteen are in the back of your lorry, and the twentieth is in the front beeping the horn."

POTENTIAL

> **"Rough diamonds may sometimes be mistaken for worthless pebbles."**
> **Sir Thomas Browne**

"Most people live, whether physically, intellectually or morally, in a very restricted circle of their potential being. They make very small use of their possible consciousness, and of their soul's resources in general, much like a man who, out of his whole bodily organism, should get into a habit of using and moving only his little finger."

William James

"Ineffective people live day after day with unused potential. They experience synergy only in small, peripheral ways in their lives. But creative experiences can be produced regularly, consistently, almost daily in people's lives. It requires enormous personal security and openness and a spirit of adventure."

Stephen R Covey

"It's the moment you think you can't, that you realise you can."

Celine Dion

"Lord, we may know what we are, but know not what we may be."

William Shakespeare

"I have always had the feeling I could do anything and my dad told me I could. I was in college before I found out he might be wrong."

Ann Richards

"The treacherous, unexplored areas of the world are not in continents or the seas; they are in the hearts and minds of men."

Allen E Claxton

"Man is as full of potential as he is of importance."

George Santayana

"I can't believe that God put us on this earth to be ordinary."

Lou Holtz

> *"I always felt that I hadn't achieved what I wanted to achieve. I always felt I could get better. That's the whole incentive."*
> **Virginia Wade**

"If you think you're too small to make a difference, you've obviously never been in bed with a mosquito."
Michelle Walker

"It's not what you've got, it's what you use that makes a difference."
Zig Ziglar

In a small village in Sweden lived a young girl who was terribly poor and unskilled, so she could get along only by doing the most menial of jobs. She loved to sing and, despite her poverty, she dreamed of some day being a great singer. She began to sing on street corners, hoping passers-by would toss her a copper or two.

Each day she sang – in wind and rain, heat or cold – yet barely had enough at the end of the day to buy food. Some in the village protested to the town council that it wasn't right for children to be on the street in rags, begging, yet no one did anything to help her.

One day, a great musician happened to pass by and hear her. He was entranced by her beautiful voice. He took the ragged urchin home with him and began to teach her how to use her glorious voice to its fullest. In time she became the toast of two continents and everyone knew and loved the "Swedish Nightingale", as they called Jenny Lind.

American artist James Whistler, who was never known to be bashful about his talent, was once advised that a shipment of blank canvases he had ordered had been lost in the mail. When asked if the canvases were of any great value, Whistler remarked, "Not yet, not yet".

When Jan Paderewski was about to leave his native Poland to play his first recital in London, he asked an influential compatriot to give him a letter of introduction to a leading figure in Britain's musical world, who might be of assistance should anything go amiss.

The letter was handed to him in a sealed envelope. He hoped that everything would proceed smoothly and he would not have to use it. He did not; his debut was a success and no snags developed.

Some years later, while going through his papers, he came upon the letter and opened it. It read: "This will introduce Jan Paderewski, who plays the piano, for which he demonstrates no conspicuous talent."

PRAYER

"When you pray, rather let your heart be without words than your words without heart."
John Bunyan

Just do your best,
Pray that it's blessed,
And He'll take care of the rest!

"Don't pray when it rains if you don't pray when the sun shines."
Satchel Paige

"There are thoughts which are prayers. There are moments when, whatever the posture of the body, the soul is on its knees."
Victor Hugo

When at night you cannot sleep, talk to the Shepherd and stop counting sheep.

"We have to pray with our eyes on God, not on the difficulties."
Oswald Chambers

"God can pick sense out of a confused prayer."
Richard Sibbes

A ship was wrecked during a storm at sea and only two of the men on it were able to swim to a small, desert-like island. The two survivors, not knowing what else to do, agreed that they had no other recourse but to pray to God.

However, to find out whose prayer was more powerful, they agreed to divide the territory between them and stay on opposite sides of the island.

The first thing they prayed for was food. The next morning, the first man saw a fruit-bearing tree on his side of the land, and he was able to eat its fruit.

The other man's parcel of land remained barren.

After a week, the first man was lonely and he decided to pray for a wife. The next day, another ship was wrecked, and the only survivor was a woman, who swam to his side of the island.

On the other side of the island, there was nothing.

Soon the first man prayed for a house, clothes and more food. The next day, like magic, all of these were given to him. However, the second man still had nothing.

Finally, the first man prayed for a ship, so that he and his wife could leave the island. In the morning, he found a ship docked at his side of the island.

The first man boarded the ship with his wife and decided to leave the second man on the island. He considered the other man unworthy to receive God's blessings, since none of his prayers had been answered.

As the ship was about to leave, the first man heard a voice from heaven booming, "Why are you leaving your companion on the island?"

"My blessings are mine alone, since I was the one who prayed for them," the first man answered. "His prayers were all unanswered and so he does not deserve anything."

"You are mistaken!" the voice rebuked him. "He had only one prayer, which I answered. If not for that, you would not have received any of my blessings."

"Tell me," the first man asked the voice, "What did he pray for that I should owe him anything?"

"He prayed that all your prayers be answered."

> As long as there are tests, there will be prayer in schools.

"Trouble and perplexity drive me to prayer, and prayer drives away perplexity and trouble."
Philip Melanchthon

"Prayer requires more of the heart than of the tongue."
Adam Clarke

"Most people do not pray; they only beg."
George Bernard Shaw

"What we usually pray to God is not that his will be done, but that he approve ours."
Helga Bergold

"Prayer is exhaling the spirit of man and inhaling the spirit of God."
Edwin Keith

"Be thankful that God's answers are wiser than your answers."
William Culbertson

"When I pray, coincidences happen. And when I stop praying, the coincidences stop."
Archbishop William Temple

Most people commit the same mistake with God that they do with their friends: they do all the talking.

"Before we can pray, 'Lord, Thy Kingdom come', we must be willing to pray, 'my Kingdom go'."
Alan Redpath

"No man ever prayed heartily without learning something."
Ralph Waldo Emerson

PREACHING

A fire-and-brimstone preacher was haranguing the congregation: "Every member of this congregation is going to die!"

But a man in the front row was grinning from ear to ear.

Again the preacher yelled: "Every member of this congregation is going to die!"

But the man starting to laugh out loud.

At the end of the service, the preacher confronted the man. "I don't get it. Every time I said every member of this congregation is going to die, you just laughed."

"Of course," replied the man. "I'm not a member of this congregation."

A minister delivered a sermon in ten minutes one Sunday morning, which was about half the usual length of his sermons.

He explained, "I regret to inform you that my dog, who is very fond of eating paper, ate that portion of my sermon which I was unable to deliver this morning."

After the service, a visitor from another church shook hands with the preacher and said, "Vicar, if that dog of yours has any pups, I want to get one to give to my minister."

A backslider suddenly began attending church faithfully on Sunday mornings, instead of going fishing as was his normal habit.

The vicar was highly gratified and, at the end of service one morning, told him, "How wonderful it makes me feel to see you at services with your good wife!"

"Well, Vicar," said the fisherman, "quite honestly, it's a matter of choice. I'd much rather hear your sermon than hers."

PRIORITIES

A couple were going on vacation, standing in line waiting to check their bags in at the airline counter.

The husband said to the wife, "I wish we had brought the piano."

The wife asked, "Why? We've got 16 bags already!"

The husband said, "Yes, I know – but the tickets are on the piano."

"We cannot decide whether or not we will live or die; we can only decide what we will die for."
Bob Pierce

Over the triple doorways of the cathedral of Milan there are three inscriptions spanning the splendid arches. Over one is carved a beautiful wreath of roses, and underneath, "All that which pleases is but for a moment".

Over the other is sculptured a cross, and there are the words, "All that which troubles us is but for a moment".

But underneath the great central entrance to the main aisle is the inscription, "That only is important which is eternal".

In Berlin Art Gallery is a painting by German painter Adolf Menzel (1815-1905). Only partially finished. Intended to show Frederick the Great speaking with some of his generals. Menzel painted generals and background, but left the king until last. He put outline of Frederick in charcoal, but died prior to finishing.

Many come to end of life without ever having put Christ into his proper place, centre stage.

A lighthouse along a bleak coast was tended by a keeper who was given enough oil for one month and told to keep the light burning every night. One day, a woman asked for oil so that her children could stay warm. Then a farmer came; his son needed oil for a lamp so he could read. Still another needed some oil for an engine. The keeper saw each as a worthy request and measured out just enough oil to satisfy all.

Near the end of the month, the tank in the lighthouse ran dry. That night the beacon was dark and three ships crashed on the rocks. More than 100 lives were lost.

When a government official investigated, the man explained what he had done and why.

"You were given one task alone," insisted the official. "It was to keep the light burning. Everything else was secondary. There is no defence."

"A weakness of all human beings," Henry Ford said, "is trying to do too many things at once. That scatters effort and destroys direction. It makes for haste, and haste makes waste. So we do things all the wrong ways possible, before we come to the right one. Then we think it is the best way because it works, and it was the only way left that we could see. Every now and then I wake up in the morning headed toward that finality, with a dozen things I want to do. I know I can't do them all at once."

When asked what he did about that, Ford replied, "I go out and trot around the house. While I'm running off the excess energy that wants to do too much, my mind clears and I see what can be done and should be done first."

"The last thing one knows is what to put first."

Pascal

Fans of the American Wild West will find in a Deadwood, South Dakota museum this inscription left by a beleaguered prospector: "I lost my gun. I lost my horse. I am out of food. The Indians are after me. But I've got all the gold I can carry!"

PROBLEMS

"You must live with people to know their problems, and live with God in order to solve them."

Peter Taylor Forsyth

"If all our misfortunes were laid in one common heap, where everyone must take an equal portion, most people would be content to take their own and depart."

Socrates

"A problem well stated is a problem half solved."

Charles Kettering

"Problems are only opportunities in work clothes."

Henry Kaiser

"Real difficulties can be overcome; it is only the imaginary ones that are unconquerable."

Theodore Vail

"The greater the difficulty, the more glory in surmounting it."

Epicurus

PROCRASTINATION

You cannot win if you do not begin.

The Procrastination Support Group meeting has been postponed!

I didn't intend to do a thing today and so far I'm right on schedule.

"Procrastination is the art of keeping up with yesterday."
Don Marquis

Only Robinson Crusoe had everything done by Friday.

"Never put off until tomorrow what you can do the day after tomorrow."
Mark Twain

"There's nothing to match curling up with a good book when there's a repair job to be done around the house."
Joe Ryan

PROGRESS

The Australian coat of arms pictures two creatures: the emu (a flightless bird) and the kangaroo. The animals were chosen because they share a characteristic that appealed to Australian citizens. Both the emu and kangaroo can move only forward, not back. The emu's three-toed foot causes it to fall if it tries to go backwards, and the kangaroo is prevented from moving in reverse by its large tail.

PROVERBS (LIFE'S MAXIMS)

The two most common elements in the universe are hydrogen and stupidity.

If at first you don't succeed, skydiving is not for you.

"Déjà moo": The feeling that you've heard this bull before.

Nothing in the known universe travels faster than a bad cheque.

A truly wise man never plays leapfrog with a unicorn.

If you are given an open-book exam, you will forget your book. Corollary: If you are given a take-home test, you will forget where you live.

The trouble with doing something right the first time is that nobody appreciates how difficult it was.

It may be that your sole purpose in life is simply to serve as a warning to others.

My law: You can't fall off the floor.

The average woman would rather have beauty than brains, because the average man can see better than he can think.

Vital papers will demonstrate their vitality by moving from where you left them to where you can't find them.

Law of Probability Distribution:
Whatever it is that hits the fan will not be evenly distributed.

PROVERBS (YIDDISH AND JEWISH)

One of life's greatest mysteries is how the boy who wasn't good enough to marry your daughter can be the father of the smartest grandchild in the world.

Better an ounce of happiness than a pound of gold.

The truly rich are those who enjoy what they have.

The door of success is marked "push" and "pull".

A mother understands what a child does not say.

Old friends, like old wines, don't lose their flavour.

What soap is to the body, laughter is to the soul.

When a habit begins to cost money, it's called a hobby.

When you're hungry, sing; when you're hurt, laugh.

PURPOSE

People without direction are a little like Alice in the fairy tale *Alice in Wonderland*. In a conversation between her and the Cheshire Cat, Alice asked, "Would you tell me, please, which way I ought to go from here?"

"That depends a good deal on where you want to get to," said the cat.

"I don't much care where," said Alice.

"Then it doesn't matter which way you go," said the cat.

"Each of our acts makes a statement as to our purpose."
Leo Buscaglia

"Purpose is the engine, the power that drives our lives."
John Noe

One of golf's immortal moments came when a Scotsman demonstrated the new game to President Ulysses Grant.

Carefully placing the ball on the tee, he took a mighty swing. The club hit the turf and scattered dirt all over the president's beard and surrounding vicinity, while the ball placidly waited on the tee.

Again the Scotsman swung, and again he missed. The president waited patiently through six tries and then quietly stated, "There seems to be a fair amount of exercise in the game, but I fail to see the purpose of the ball."

QUESTIONS

Is the hardness of the butter proportional to the softness of the bread?

In hospital, why do they wake you up to give you a sleeping tablet?

If time heals all wounds, how come the belly button always stays the same?

Is experience what you get when you don't get what you want?

When travelling at the speed of sound, can you still hear the radio?

Why do they sell charcoal briquettes at petrol stations?

Why do teenagers express their burning desire to be different by dressing exactly the same?

Star Wars starts, "A long time ago, in a galaxy far away..." – yet how come everything is so futuristic?

When you've lost something, and ask somebody else if they've seen it, why do they always say, "Where did you leave it?"
   If you knew where you left it, it wouldn't be lost.

Is there a word for "sand" in the Icelandic dictionary?

Why is the phrase "It's none of my business" always followed by "but…"?

If Spiderman became arachnophobic would he be scared of himself?

I really resonate with Spidey's story there. Used to be that the bat was a real source of inspiration to me....

QUICK ANSWERS

The cop got out of his car and the kid who was stopped for speeding rolled down his window.

"I've been waiting for you all day," the cop said.

The kid replied, "Yeah, well I got here as fast as I could."

When the cop finally stopped laughing, he sent the kid on his way without a ticket.

A lady was picking through the frozen turkeys at the grocery store, but couldn't find one big enough for her family. She asked a stock boy, "Do these turkeys get any bigger?"

The stock boy replied, "No, ma'am, they're dead."

A truck driver is driving along on the freeway. A sign comes up that reads, "Low bridge ahead". Before he knows it, the bridge is right ahead of him and he gets stuck under the bridge. Cars are backed up for miles.

Finally, a police car comes up.

The cop gets out of his car and walks around to the truck driver, puts his hands on his hips and says, "Got stuck, huh?"

The truck driver says, "No, I was delivering this bridge and ran out of gas."

A girl was visiting her blonde friend who had acquired two new dogs, and asked her what their names were. The blonde responded by saying that one was named Rolex and one was named Timex.

Her friend said, "Whoever heard of someone naming dogs like that?"

"Hellooooooooooooooooooooooooooooooo," answered the blonde. "They're watch dogs!"

QUILTING

Quilting with a friend will keep you in stitches.

When life gives you scraps – make a quilt.

May your sorrows be patched and your joys quilted.

Those who sleep under a quilt sleep under a blanket of love.

Our lives are like quilts: bits and pieces, joy and sorrow, stitched with love.

REPENTANCE

A man volunteered to paint the church steeple. With great difficulty, he hoisted himself up onto the steeple with a can of paint and a bottle of water.

After painting half the steeple, the man realised that he was running out of paint, so he added some of the water to the paint. He was almost at the top when he realised he needed more paint to finish, so he added more water to the paint, and mumbled, "No one will ever know."

When he finished painting, he began to lower himself off the steeple.

Just then, the skies darkened, a loud clap of thunder was heard, and a deep voice from above said, "Repaint, repaint, and thin no more!"

RESPONSIBILITY

The sales manager of a dog food company asked his sales team how they liked the company's new advertising campaign.

"Great, the best in the business," they replied.

"How do you like our new label and the package?"

"Great, the best in the business," they replied.

"How do you like our sales force?" They *were* the sales force so they had to admit they were good.

"OK then," said the manager. "So we've got the best label, the best package, the best advertising program being sold by the best sales team in the business. Tell me, why are we in 17th place in the dog food business?"

There was silence... Finally someone said, "It's those lousy dogs. They won't eat the stuff!"

RESURRECTION

A man goes on vacation to the Holy Land with his wife and mother-in-law. The mother-in-law dies.

They go to an undertaker, who explains that they can ship the body home but that it'll cost over $5,000, whereas they can bury her in the Holy Land for only $150.

The man says, "We'll ship her home."

The undertaker asks, "Are you sure? That's an awfully big expense and we can do a very nice burial here."

The man says, "Look, 2,000 years ago they buried a guy here and three days later he rose from the dead. I just can't take that chance."

RUGBY

An American decided to write a book about famous churches around the world. So he bought a plane ticket and took a trip to Orlando, thinking that he would start by working his way across the USA from south to north.

On his first day he was inside a church taking photographs when he noticed a golden telephone mounted on the wall with a sign that read "$10,000 per call". The American, being intrigued, asked a priest who was strolling by what the telephone was used for. The priest replied that it was a direct line to heaven and that for $10,000 you could talk to God.

The American thanked the priest and went on his way.

Next stop was in Atlanta. There, in a very large cathedral, he saw the same golden telephone with the same sign under it. He wondered if this was the same kind of telephone he had seen in Orlando, so he asked a nearby nun what its purpose was. She told him that it was a direct line to heaven and that for $10,000 he could talk to God. "OK, thank you," said the American.

He then travelled to Indianapolis, Washington DC, Philadelphia, Boston, and New York. In every church he saw the same golden telephone with the same "$10,000 per call" sign under it.

The American, upon leaving Vermont, decided to travel across the Atlantic to see if the English had the same phone. He arrived in London and, before starting his tour of churches, decided to drop into Twickenham to visit the stadium and get a feel for this rugby football that he'd heard so much about. He took the stadium tour and was surprised to see the same golden telephone, but this time the sign under it read "10 pence per call". The American was surprised, so he asked the tour guide about the sign.

"I've travelled all over America and I've seen this same golden telephone in many churches. I'm told that it is a direct line to heaven, but in the US the price was $10,000 per call. Why is it so cheap here?"

The priest smiled and answered, "You're at Twickenham now, son – it's a local call."

SANTA

"Let me see if I've got this Santa business straight. You say he wears a beard, has no discernible source of income and flies to cities all over the world under cover of darkness? You sure this guy isn't laundering illegal drug money?"
Tom Armstrong

"Does Santa call his elves 'subordinate clauses'?"
Doug Hecox

It's all here— make the swap

"I stopped believing in Santa Claus when I was six. Mother took me to see him in a department store and he asked for my autograph."

Shirley Temple

"I never believed in Santa Claus because I knew no white man would be coming into my neighbourhood after dark."

Dick Gregory

"Santa Claus wears a red suit;
He must be a communist.
And a beard and long hair;
Must be a pacifist.
What's in that pipe that he's
   smoking?"

Arlo Guthrie

"Santa Claus has the right idea. Visit people once a year."
Victor Borge

"Yes, Virginia, there is a Santa Claus... Thank God! He lives, and he lives forever. A thousand years from now, Virginia, nay, ten times ten thousand years from now, he will continue to make glad the heart of childhood."

Francis Pharcellus Church,
The Sun, 21 September 1897

"I played Santa Claus many times, and if you don't believe it, check out the divorce settlements awarded my wives."
Groucho Marx, *The Groucho Phile*

"Santa is even-tempered. Santa does not hit children over the head who kick him. Santa uses the term 'folks' rather than Mommy and Daddy because of all the broken homes. Santa does not have a three-martini lunch. Santa does not borrow money from store employees. Santa wears a good deodorant."
Jenny Zink (to employees of Western Temporary Services, the world's largest supplier of Santa Clauses, *New York Times,* 21 November 1984)

SECRETARIES

The secretary's prayer

Dear Lord,

I NEED HELP. Help me to be a good secretary, and help me to have the memory of an elephant, or one at least three years long. Help me by some miracle to be able to do six things at once, to answer four telephones at the same time while typing a letter that must go out today. And, when that letter doesn't get signed until tomorrow, give me the strength to keep from going over the brink of hysteria. Never let me lose patience, even when the boss has me searching the files for hours for data that is later discovered in his desk.

HELP ME to have the intelligence of a college professor; help me to understand and carry out all instructions without being given clear explanations. Let me know always just where the boss is, even though he left without telling me where he was going. And when the year ends, please let me have the foresight not to destroy records that will be asked for in a few weeks, even though I was told to destroy them all.

HELP ME to keep a level head and my feet on the ground, so that my secretarial performance will be a proper reflection of the pioneer women who made a place for me in the business world, and those who established me in a profession.

SELF-WORTH

Below is an actual essay written by a college applicant:

In order for the admissions staff at our college to get to know you, the applicant, better, we ask that you answer the following question: Are there any significant experiences you have had, or accomplishments you have realised, that have helped to define you as a person?

I am a dynamic figure, often seen scaling walls and crushing ice. I have been known to remodel train stations on my lunch breaks, making them more efficient in the area of heat retention. I translate ethnic slurs for Cuban refugees, I write award-winning operas, I manage time efficiently. Occasionally, I tread water for three days in a row.

I woo women with my sensuous and godlike trombone-playing, I can pilot bicycles up severe inclines with unflagging speed, and I cook 30-minute brownies in 20 minutes. I am an expert in stucco, a veteran in love, and an outlaw in Peru.

Using only a hoe and a large glass of water, I once single-handedly defended a small village in the Amazon Basin from a horde of ferocious army ants. I play bluegrass cello, I was scouted by the Mets, I am the subject of numerous documentaries. When I'm bored, I build large suspension bridges in my yard. I enjoy urban hang-gliding. On Wednesdays after school, I repair electrical appliances free of charge.

I am an abstract artist, a concrete analyst, and a

ruthless bookie. Critics worldwide swoon over my original line of corduroy evening wear. I don't perspire. I am a private citizen, yet I receive fan mail. I have been caller number nine and have won the weekend passes. Last summer I toured New Jersey with a travelling centrifugal-force demonstration. I bat .400. My deft floral arrangements have earned me fame in international botany circles. Children trust me.

I can hurl tennis rackets at small moving objects with deadly accuracy. I once read *Paradise Lost*, *Moby Dick* and *David Copperfield* in one day and still had time to refurbish an entire dining room that evening. I know the exact location of every food item in the supermarket. I have performed several covert operations for the CIA. I sleep once a week; when I do sleep, I sleep in a chair. While on vacation in Canada, I successfully negotiated with a group of terrorists who had seized a small bakery. The law of physics does not apply to me.

I balance, I weave, I dodge, I frolic, and my bills are all paid. On weekends, to let off steam, I participate in full-contact origami. Years ago I discovered the meaning of life but forgot to write it down. I have made extraordinary four-course meals using only a mouli and a toaster oven. I breed prizewinning clams. I have won bullfights in San Juan, cliff-diving competitions in Sri Lanka, and spelling bees at the Kremlin. I have played Hamlet, I have performed open-heart surgery and I have spoken with Elvis.

But I have not yet gone to college.

At the Pan American Games, Greg Louganis was asked how he coped with the stress of the international diving competition. He replied that he climbs to the board, takes a deep breath, and thinks, "Even if I blow this dive, my mother will still love me." Then he goes for excellence.

At the beginning of each day, how good it would be for each of us to take a deep breath, say, "Even if I blow this dive, my Father in heaven will still love me", and then, assured of grace, go into the day seeking a perfect "10"!

Once, walking through the twisted little streets of Kowloon in Hong Kong, I came upon a tattoo studio. In the window were displayed samples of the tattoos available. On the chest or arms you could have tattooed an anchor or flag or mermaid or whatever. But what struck me with force were three words that could be tattooed on one's flesh: Born to lose. I entered the shop in astonishment and, pointing to those words, asked the Chinese tattoo artist, "Does anyone really have that terrible phrase, Born to lose, tattooed on his body?"

He replied, "Yes, sometimes."

"But," I said, "I just can't believe that anyone in his right mind would do that."

The Chinese man simply tapped his forehead and said in broken English, "Before tattoo on body, tattoo on mind."

Norman Vincent Peal

Charlie Chaplin once entered a Charlie Chaplin lookalike contest in Monte Carlo – and came in third.

SERVICE

Waiter's unusual donation

A waiter at a hotel in Hawaii has been named employee of the year after donating a kidney to a regular customer. Walter Nishioka, 70, a local businessman, was seriously ill with kidney disease and had been told that he needed a transplant urgently. But doctors could not find him a donor – until Jose Rocasa, 52, a waiter at the Radisson Prince Kuhio on Waikiki Beach, offered one of his own. Nishioka had eaten brunch at the hotel every Wednesday for the past 22 years, and had always been a generous tipper. Rocasa's boss described him as "a server who became a saviour".

> "What is it to serve God and to do his will? Nothing else than to show mercy to our neighbour. For it is our neighbour who needs our service; God in heaven needs it not."
> **Martin Luther**

SIGNS

Lightning hits preacher after call to God

A congregation in the United States was left stunned when lightning struck a church moments after a visiting preacher asked God for a sign.

Church members in the town of Forest in the state of Ohio said the preacher had been emphasising the importance of penance when, in the course of his prayers, he called on the heavens above.

The lightning struck the steeple, then hit the preacher himself when it travelled through electrical wiring to his microphone.

Local authorities said he was not injured.

"It was awesome, just awesome," said church member Ronnie Cheney, who was among the congregation when the strike hit, to the *Findlay Courier* newspaper.

"You could hear the storm building outside…he just kept asking God what else he needed to say. He was asking for a sign and he got one."

Afterwards services resumed; however, churchgoers realised after 20 minutes that the building was on fire and evacuated.

"It was kind of interesting hearing the preacher talk about what had happened," Forest Fire Chief Doug Hawkin admitted.

The fire was put out after three hours, but damage to the church is estimated at around $20,000.

Story from BBC NEWS: Published: 2003/07/04 10:47:38 GMT

SILENCE

"Silence has many dimensions. It can be a regression and an escape, a loss of self, or it can be presence, awareness, unification, self-discovery.

Negative silence blurs and confuses our identity, and we lapse into daydreams or diffuse anxieties. Positive silence pulls us together and makes us realise who we are, who we might be, and the distance between these two. Hence, positive silence implies a disciplined choice, and what Paul Tillich called the 'courage to be'. In the long run, the discipline of creative silence demands a certain kind of faith. For when we come face to face with ourselves in the lonely ground of our own being, we confront many questions about the value of our existence, the reality of our commitments, the authenticity of our everyday lives."

Thomas Merton

STRESS

All stressed up and nowhere to go.

I don't suffer from stress. I am a carrier.

I feel stress at only two times – day and night!

Stressed is desserts spelled backwards.

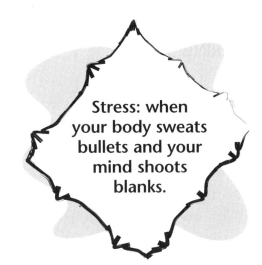

Stress: when your body sweats bullets and your mind shoots blanks.

STUPIDITY

The following examples of heroic stupidity have recently come up for a special award:

When his 38-calibre revolver failed to fire at his intended victim during a hold-up in Long Beach, California, would-be robber James Elliot did something that can only inspire wonder. He peered down the barrel and tried the trigger again. This time it worked…

An American teenager was in the hospital recovering from serious head wounds received from an oncoming train. When asked how he received the injuries, the lad told police that he was simply trying to see how close he could get his head to a moving train before he was hit.

As a female shopper exited a New York convenience store, a man grabbed her purse and ran. The clerk called 911 immediately, and the woman was able to give them a detailed description of the snatcher. Within minutes, the police apprehended the snatcher. They put him in the car and drove back to the store. The thief was then taken out of the car and told to stand there for a positive ID. To which he replied, "Yes, officer, that's her. That's the lady I stole the purse from."

The *Ann Arbor News* crime column reported that a man walked into a Burger King in Ypsilanti, Michigan, at 5 am, flashed a gun, and demanded cash. The clerk turned him down because he said he couldn't open the cash register without a food order. When the man ordered onion rings, the clerk said they weren't available for breakfast. The man, frustrated, walked away.

When a man attempted to siphon gasoline from a motor home parked on a Seattle street, he got much more than he bargained for. Police arrived at the scene to find a very sick man curled up next to a motor home near spilled sewage. A police spokesman said that the man admitted to trying to steal gasoline and plugged his siphon hose into the motor home's sewage tank by mistake. The owner of the vehicle declined to press charges, saying that it was the best laugh he'd ever had.

SUFFERING

"Comfort and prosperity have never enriched the world as much as adversity has. Out of pain and problems have come the sweetest songs, and the most gripping stories."

Billy Graham

TAX

A dad walks into a market followed by his ten-year-old son. The kid is spinning a 20-pence piece in the air and catching it between his teeth. As they walk through the market someone bumps into the boy at just the wrong moment and the coin goes straight into his mouth and lodges in his throat.

He immediately starts choking and going blue in the face and Dad starts panicking, shouting and screaming for help.

A middle-aged, fairly unnoticeable man in a grey suit is sitting at a coffee bar in the market reading his newspaper and sipping a cup of coffee. At the sound of the commotion he looks up, puts his coffee cup down on the saucer, neatly folds his newspaper and places it on the counter. He gets up from his seat and makes his unhurried way across the market. Reaching the boy (who is still standing, but only just) the man carefully takes hold of the kid's balls and squeezes gently but firmly. After a few seconds the boy convulses violently and coughs up the 20-pence piece, which the man catches in his free hand.

Releasing the boy, the man hands the coin to the father and walks back to his seat in the coffee bar without saying a word. As soon as he is sure that his son has suffered no lasting ill-effects, the father rushes over to the man and starts thanking him. The man looks embarrassed and brushes off the father's thanks.

As he's about to leave, the father asks one last question: "I've never seen anybody do anything like that before – it was fantastic – what are you, a surgeon or something like that?"

"Oh, good heavens, no," the man replies. "I work for the Inland Revenue."

TEETH

A dinner speaker was in such a hurry to get to his engagement that when he arrived and sat down at the head table, he suddenly realised that he had forgotten his false teeth. Turning to the man next to him he said, "I forgot my teeth."

The man said, "No problem". He reached into his pocket and pulled out a pair of false teeth. "Try these," he said. The speaker tried them. "Too loose," he said.

The man then said, "I have another pair – try these." The speaker tried them and responded, "Too tight".

The man was not taken aback at all. He then said, "I have one more pair. Try them." The speaker said, "They fit perfectly." With that, he ate his meal and gave his speech.

After the dinner meeting was over, the speaker went over to thank the man who had helped him. "I want to thank you for coming to my aid. Where is your office? I've been looking for a good dentist."

The man replied, "Oh, I'm not a dentist. I'm an undertaker."

TEMPTATION

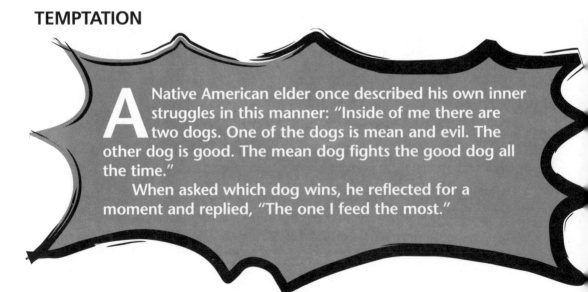

A Native American elder once described his own inner struggles in this manner: "Inside of me there are two dogs. One of the dogs is mean and evil. The other dog is good. The mean dog fights the good dog all the time."

When asked which dog wins, he reflected for a moment and replied, "The one I feed the most."

"Do not bite at the bait of pleasure till you know there is no hook."
Thomas Jefferson

"Few men have virtue to withstand the highest bidder."
George Washington

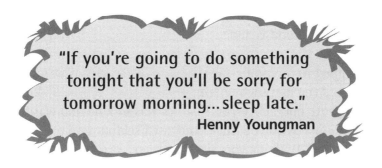

"If you're going to do something tonight that you'll be sorry for tomorrow morning... sleep late."
Henny Youngman

THANKSGIVING

"Be thankful for what you have; you'll end up having more. If you concentrate on what you don't have, you will never, ever have enough."
Oprah Winfrey

"Gratitude is not only the greatest of virtues, but the parent of all the others."
Cicero

"No duty is more urgent than that of returning thanks."
Saint Ambrose

"Silent gratitude isn't very much use to anyone."
Gladys Stern

"Thou hast given me so much… Give me one thing more, a grateful heart."
George Herbert

Forgive Me When I Whine

Today upon a bus I saw a lovely maid with golden hair;
I envied her – she seemed so happy, and how I wished I were so fair;
When suddenly she rose to leave, I saw her hobble down the aisle;
She had one foot and wore a crutch, but as she passed, a smile.
Oh, God, forgive me when I whine,
I have two feet – the world is mine.

And when I stopped to buy some sweets,
The lad who served me had such charm;
He seemed to radiate good cheer, his manner was so kind and warm;
I said, "It's nice to deal with you, such courtesy I seldom find";
He turned and said, "Oh, thank you, sir", and then I saw that he was blind.
Oh, God, forgive me when I whine,
I have two eyes – the world is mine.

Then, when walking down the street, I saw a child with eyes of blue;
He stood and watched the others play, it seemed he knew not what to do;
I stopped a moment, then I said, "Why don't you join the others, dear?"
He looked ahead without a word, and then I knew he could not hear.
Oh, God, forgive me when I whine,
I have two ears – the world is mine.

With feet to take me where I'd go,
With eyes to see the sunset's glow,
With ears to hear what I would know,
I'm blessed indeed – the world is mine;
Oh, God, forgive me when I whine.

When eating fruit, think of the person who planted the tree.
Vietnamese proverb

Why did only one cleansed leper return to thank Jesus? The following are nine suggested reasons why the nine did not return:

One waited to see if the cure was real.
One waited to see if it would last.
One said he would see Jesus later.
One decided that he had never had leprosy.
One said he would have got well anyway.
One gave thanks to the priests.
One said, "Oh, well, Jesus didn't really do anything."
One said, "Any rabbi could have done it."
One said, "I was already much improved."

In his book *Folk Psalms of Faith*, Ray Stedman tells of an experience H A Ironside had in a crowded restaurant.

Just as Ironside was about to begin his meal, a man approached and asked if he could join him. Ironside invited him to have a seat. Then, as was his custom, Ironside bowed his head in prayer. When he opened his eyes, the other man asked, "Do you have a headache?" Ironside replied, "No, I don't."

The other man asked, "Well, is there something wrong with your food?" Ironside replied, "No, I was simply thanking God as I always do before I eat."

The man said, "Oh, you're one of those, are you? Well, I want you to know I never give thanks. I earn my money by the sweat of my brow and I don't have to give thanks to anybody when I eat. I just start right in!"

Ironside said, "Yes, you're just like my dog. That's what he does too!"

A twelve-year-old boy named David had been born without an immune system. He underwent a bone-marrow transplant in order to correct the deficiency. Up to that point he had spent his entire life in a plastic bubble in order to prevent exposure to common germs, bacteria and viruses that could kill him. He lived without ever knowing human contact. When asked what he'd like to do if and when released from his protective bubble, he replied, "I want to walk barefoot on grass, and touch my mother's hand."

In a sermon at Immanuel Presbyterian Church in Los Angeles, Gary Wilburn said, "In 1636, amid the darkness of the Thirty Years' War, a German pastor, Martin Rinkart, is said to have buried 5,000 of his parishioners in one year, an average of fifteen a day. His parish was ravaged by war, death, and economic disaster. In the heart of that darkness, with the cries of fear outside his window, he sat down and wrote this table grace for his children:

Now thank we all our God
With heart and hands and voices;
Who wondrous things hath done,
In whom His world rejoices.
Who, from our mother's arms,
Hath led us on our way
With countless gifts of love
And still is ours today.

Here was a man who knew thanksgiving comes from love of God, not from outward circumstances."

In Budapest, a man goes to a rabbi and complains, "Life is unbearable. There are nine of us living in one room. What can I do?"

The rabbi answers, "Take your goat into the room with you." The man is incredulous, but the rabbi insists, "Do as I say and come back in a week."

A week later the man comes back, looking more distraught than before. "We cannot stand it," he tells the rabbi. "The goat is filthy."

The rabbi then tells him, "Go home and let the goat out. And come back in a week."

A radiant man returns to the rabbi a week later, exclaiming, "Life is beautiful. We enjoy every minute of it now that there's no goat – only the nine of us."

> Scottish minister Alexander Whyte was known for his uplifting prayers in the pulpit. He always found something for which to be grateful. One Sunday morning the weather was so gloomy that one church member thought to himself, "Certainly the preacher won't think of anything for which to thank the Lord on a wretched day like this." Much to his surprise, however, Whyte began by praying, "We thank thee, O God, that it is not always like this."

TIME

You can't make footprints in the sands of time sitting down.

"You may delay, but time will not."
Benjamin Franklin

"Time is what we want most, but what we use worst."
William Penn

"Time is but the stream I go a-fishing in."
Henry David Thoreau

"I wish I could stand on a busy corner, hat in hand, and beg people to throw me all their wasted hours."
Bernard Berenson

Don't say you don't have enough time. You have exactly the same number of hours per day that were given to Helen Keller, Leonardo da Vinci, Thomas Jefferson, and Albert Einstein.

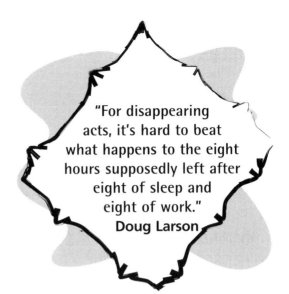

"For disappearing acts, it's hard to beat what happens to the eight hours supposedly left after eight of sleep and eight of work."
Doug Larson

TOURISM

The Tourist's Prayer

Heavenly Father, look down on us, your obedient servants, who are doomed to travel this earth taking photos, writing postcards, buying souvenirs and walking around in drip-dry underwear.

We beseech you, O Lord, to see that our plane is not delayed, our baggage not lost and our overweight luggage and illegal imports are unnoticed...

Lead us to good inexpensive restaurants where the wine is included in the price of the meal and the staff speaks our tongue. Give us the wisdom to tip correctly in currencies we do not understand.

Grant us the strength to visit museums, palaces, cathedrals and if per chance we skip an historic monument to seek private pleasure, have mercy on us, for our flesh is weak.

Dear God, protect our wives from bargains they do not need, or cannot afford. Lead them not into temptation, for they know not what they do.

Almighty Father, keep our husbands from looking at foreign women and comparing them with us. Save them from making fools of themselves at social gatherings. Above all, do not forgive them their trespasses, for they know exactly what they do.

And finally, when our wanderings are over, grant us the favour of finding someone who will look at our videos and photos and listen to our prattle, so that our journey has not been in vain.

TROUBLES

"Tough times don't last. Tough people do."
Robert Schuller

"My mum said to me very early – 'Son, if they don't like you, they've got bad taste.'"
Bob Hoskins, actor

The light at the end of the tunnel is an oncoming train.

"Fall seven times; stand up eight."
Japanese proverb

"I ask not for a lighter burden, but for broader shoulders."
Jewish proverb

The company you keep will determine the trouble you meet.

"The only difference between the big shot and the little shot is that the big shot was simply the little shot that kept shooting."
Zig Ziglar

Sometimes the littlest things in life are the hardest to take. You can sit on a mountain more comfortably than on a tack.

"Every path has its puddle."
English proverb

"When it is dark enough, you can see the stars."
Ralph Waldo Emerson

It just wouldn't be a picnic without the ants.

The first rule of holes: If you are in one, stop digging.

"For sleep, riches and health to be truly enjoyed, they must be interrupted."

Jean Paul Richter

"He who has a 'why' to live can bear almost any 'how.'"

Friedrich Nietzsche

"There is no education like adversity."

Disraeli

"Don't think there are no crocodiles because the water is calm."

Malayan proverb

You can tell a lot about a person by the way they handle these three things: a rainy day, lost luggage, and tangled Christmas tree lights.

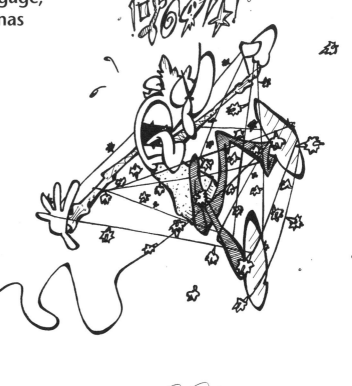

For every cloud there's a silver lining,
for every valley there's a hill,
for every challenge...
there's a corny cliché!

"When solving problems, dig at the roots instead of just hacking at the leaves."
Anthony J D'Angelo

"You must have chaos within you to give birth to a dancing star."
Nietzsche

"People who invite trouble always complain when it accepts."
Lane Olinghouse

"In the depth of winter I finally learned that there was in me an invincible summer."
Albert Camus

TRUISMS

How come it takes so little time for a child who is afraid of the dark to become a teenager who wants to stay out all night?

Business conventions are important because they demonstrate how many people a company can operate without.

Think about this... No one ever says, "It's only a game", when their team is winning.

If you don't have a sense of humour, you probably don't have any sense at all.

Always keep your words soft and sweet, just in case you have to eat them.

Drive carefully.
It's not only cars that can be recalled by their maker.

TRUTH

"It's discouraging to think how many people are shocked by honesty and how few by deceit."

Noël Coward

"Truth is stranger than fiction, but it is because fiction is obliged to stick to possibilities; truth isn't."
Mark Twain

"The highest compact we can make with our fellow is, 'Let there be truth between us two for evermore.'"
Ralph Waldo Emerson

UNDERSTANDING

A man was on the side of the road hitchhiking on a very dark night and in the middle of a storm. The night was rolling on and no car went by. The storm was so strong he could hardly see a few feet ahead of him.

Suddenly he saw a car coming toward him and stop.

Without thinking about it, the man got into the back seat, closed the door and then realised there was nobody behind the wheel! The car started slowly; the man looked at the road and saw a curve coming his way. Scared, he started to pray, begging for his life. He hadn't come out of shock when, just before he hit the curve, a hand appeared through the window and moved the wheel. The man, paralysed in terror, watched how the hand appeared every time, right before a curve.

Gathering his strength, the man finally jumped out of the car and ran to the nearest town. Wet and in shock, he went to a restaurant and started telling everybody about the horrible experience he had been through.

A silence enveloped everybody when they realised the man was serious.

About half an hour later, two men walked into the same restaurant.

As they looked around for a table, one said to the other, "Look John, that's the man who got in the car when we were pushing it."

UNSELFISHNESS

Years ago, the Salvation Army was holding an international convention and their founder, General William Booth, could not attend because of physical weakness. He cabled his convention message to them. It was one word: "OTHERS".

VALENTINES

These are entries to a competition asking for a rhyme with the most romantic first line but least romantic second line:

I thought that I could love no other,
Until, that is, I met your brother

Roses are red, violets are blue, sugar is sweet, and so are you.
But the roses are wilting, the violets are dead, the sugar
bowl's empty and so is your head.

Of loving beauty you float with grace,
If only you could hide your face.

Kind, intelligent, loving and hot,
This describes everything you are not.

I want to feel your sweet embrace,
But don't take that paper bag off your face.

I love your smile, your face, and your eyes –
Damn, I'm good at telling lies!

My darling, my lover, my beautiful wife:
Marrying you screwed up my life.

I see your face when I am dreaming,
That's why I always wake up screaming.

What inspired this amorous rhyme?
Two parts vodka, one part lime.

VETS

A man takes his Rottweiler to the vet. "My dog's cross-eyed. Is there anything you can do for him?"

"Well," says the vet, "let's have a look at him." So he picks the dog up and examines his eyes, then checks his teeth. Finally he says, "I'm going to have to put him down."

"What? Because he's cross-eyed?"

"No, because he's really heavy."

VICARS

There was once a very rough Parish Church Council meeting. Strong opinions were expressed and sharp disagreements surfaced.

The next day one of the PCC members felt bad about the whole meeting, and asked the vicar if he had slept well after the meeting had ended.

He replied, "I slept like a baby."

"Really?"

"Yes, I woke up every hour crying!"

It's nice to work for the Lord. The pay isn't much but the retirement plan is out of this world!

Old ministers never die, they just go out to pastor!

VOLUNTEERS

Those who can, do.
Those who can do more, volunteer!

Volunteers are
love in motion!

"Volunteers do not
necessarily have
the time; they just
have the heart."
Elizabeth Andrew

Volunteers don't get paid, not
because they're worthless, but
because they're priceless!

WEATHER

Weather bulletin, broadcast by a TV station: "Severe thunderstorm coming. Stay inside. Do not use any electrical appliances. Stay tuned for further information."

> Q: **What normally follows two days of rain?**
> A: **Monday**

WEDDINGS

*To have and to hold,
to love and to cherish,
from this day forward…*

> Dance through life with me – the best is yet to be.

"What's the earth with all its art, verse, music worth – compared with love, found, gained, and kept?"
Robert Browning

The joining of two hands makes one heart!

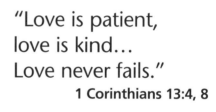

"Love is patient, love is kind… Love never fails."
1 Corinthians 13:4, 8

Loving you is a wonderful way to spend a lifetime!

"What greater thing is there for two human souls than to feel that they are joined for life."
George Eliot

"God is a great matchmaker."
Jewish proverb

"Love is a flower which turns into fruit at marriage."

Finnish proverb

Life is a journey, and I'm so glad we're travelling together!

We may not have it all together, but together we have it all.

Let our love be like
an arch:
two weaknesses
learning together to
form one strength.

Two hearts
once joined in
friendship,
united now
with love.

"And now abide faith, hope, and love, these
three; but the greatest of these is love."
1 Corinthians 13:13, New King James Version

"God, the best maker of all marriages, Combine your hearts into one."

William Shakespeare

"What therefore God has joined together, let no man put asunder."

Mark 10:9

When Adam was lonely, God created for him not ten friends, but one wife.

Henceforth there shall be such a oneness between you, that when one weeps, the other will taste salt.

TWENTY RULES OF WISDOM

1. God wants spiritual fruit, not religious nuts.
2. Dear God, I have a problem; it's me.
3. Growing old is inevitable, growing UP is optional.
4. There is no key to happiness. The door is always open.
5. Silence is often misinterpreted, but never misquoted.
6. You do the maths. Count your blessings.
7. Faith is the ability to not panic.
8. Laugh every day; it's like inner jogging.
9. If you worry, don't pray. If you pray…don't worry.
10. As a child of God, prayer is kind of like calling home every day.
11. Blessed are the flexible for they shall not be bent out of shape.
12. The most important things in your home are the people!
13. When we get tangled up in our problems, be still; God wants us to be still so he can untangle the knot.

14. A grudge is a heavy thing to carry.
15. He who dies with the most toys is still dead.
16. We do not remember days, but moments. Life is moving too fast – so enjoy your precious moments.
17. Nothing is real to you until you experience it; otherwise, it's just hearsay.
18. It's all right to sit on your pity pot every now and again. Just be sure to flush when you are done.
19. Surviving and living your life successfully requires courage. The goals and dreams you're seeking require courage and risk-taking. Learn from the turtle: it only makes progress when it sticks out its neck.
20. Be more concerned with your character than your reputation, because your character is what you really are, while your reputation is merely what others think you are.

"If 50 million people say a foolish thing, it is still a foolish thing."
Anatole France

WISHES

A man walks up to a bar with an ostrich behind him and, as he sits, the bartender comes over and asks for their order. The man says, "I'll have a beer" and turns to the ostrich: "What's yours?"

"I'll have a beer, too," says the ostrich.

The bartender pours the beer and says, "That will be $3.40, please." The man reaches into his pocket and pulls out the exact change for payment.

The next day, the man and the ostrich come to the bar again and the man says, "I'll have a beer" and the ostrich says, "I'll have the same." Once again the man reaches into his pocket and pays with exact change.

This becomes a routine until, late one evening, the two enter again.

"The usual?" asks the bartender.

"Well, it's close to last call, so I'll have a large Scotch," says the man.

"Same for me," says the ostrich.

"That will be $7.20," says the bartender. Once again the man pulls the exact change out of his pocket and places it on the bar. The bartender can't hold back his curiosity any longer.

"Excuse me, sir. How do you manage to always come up with the exact change out of your pocket every time?"

"Well," says the man, "several years ago I was cleaning the attic and I found an old lamp. When I rubbed it a genie appeared and offered me two wishes. My first wish was that if I ever have to pay for anything, I just put my hand in my pocket and the right amount of money will always be there."

"That's brilliant!" says the bartender. "Most people would wish for a million dollars or something, but you'll always be as rich as you want for as long as you live!"

"That's right! Whether it's a pint of milk or a Rolls Royce, the exact money is always there," says the man.

The bartender asks, "One other thing, sir…what's with the ostrich?"

The man replies, "My second wish was for a chick with long legs."

WOMEN

A man walking along a California beach was deep in prayer. All of a sudden, he said out loud, "Lord, grant me one wish."

The sky clouded above his head and, in a booming voice, the Lord said, "Because you have tried to be faithful to me in all ways, I will grant you one wish."

The man said, "Build a bridge to Hawaii so I can drive over any time I want."

The Lord said, "Your request is very materialistic. Think of the enormous challenges for that kind of undertaking. The supports required to reach the bottom of the Pacific! The concrete and steel it would take!

I can do it, but it is hard for me to justify your desire for worldly things. Take a little more time and think of another wish, a wish you think would honour and glorify me."

The man thought about it for a long time.

Finally he said, "Lord, I wish that I could understand women. I want to know how they feel inside, what they are thinking when they give the silent treatment, why they cry, what they mean when they say 'nothing', and how I can make a woman truly happy."

The Lord replied, "You want two lanes or four lanes on that bridge?"

WORK

Out of 132 public episodes in the Gospels, 122 are in the marketplace.

Out of 52 parables Jesus told, 45 had a workplace context.

Out of 40 miracles in the book of Acts, 39 were in the marketplace.

Jesus spent more than 50% of his life as a carpenter before he began preaching.

I owe, I owe, it's off to work I go.

Tell your boss what you think of him and the truth shall set you free.

Just when you thought you were winning the rat race, along come faster rats.

We, the unwilling, led by the unqualified, are doing the impossible for the ungrateful.

"Nothing is impossible for the man who doesn't have to do it himself."
A H Weiler

"When work is a pleasure, life is a joy! When work is a duty, life is slavery."
Maxim Gorky

"If you aren't fired with enthusiasm, you will be fired with enthusiasm."
Vince Lombardi

All I want is less to do, more time to do it, and higher pay for not getting it done.

The only place success comes before work is in the dictionary.

"If a man is called to be a street sweeper, he should sweep streets even as Michelangelo painted, or Beethoven composed music, or Shakespeare wrote poetry. He should sweep streets so well that all the host of heaven and earth will pause to say: Here lived a great street sweeper who did his job well."
Dr Martin Luther King, Jr

WORRY

Worry is like a rocking chair; it gives you something to do but doesn't get you anywhere.

"How much pain they have cost us, the evils which have never happened."

Thomas Jefferson

"I am an old man and have known a great many troubles, but most of them never happened."

Mark Twain

"We probably wouldn't worry about what people think of us if we could know how seldom they do."

Olin Miller

"To him who is in fear everything rustles."

Sophocles

"Rule number one is, don't sweat the small stuff. Rule number two is, it's all small stuff."

Robert Eliot

WORSHIP

Through her parents' divorce, her struggle with bulimia, and her miscarriage, Australian worship leader Darlene Zschech found a secret weapon for survival: worship.

Australian worship leader Darlene Zschech didn't set out to write a globally popular praise song when she penned "Shout to the Lord" in 1993. "I wrote it when I was feeling discouraged," explains the 35-year-old Queensland native. "I felt I could either scream and pull my hair out – or praise God."

At the time, Darlene and her husband, Mark, had two babies and, with a struggling motorcycle-parts business, money was tight. It was during one particularly stressful day that Darlene snuck into a room where they kept their piano and put into song the spiritual truths to which she desperately clung: "Mountains bow down and the seas will roar at the sound of your name" and "Nothing compares to the promise I have in you".

"We sing 'Make a joyful noise to the Lord' while our faces reflect the sadness of one who has just buried a rich aunt who left everything to her pregnant hamster."
Erma Bombeck

XMAS

Many people think that it's wrong to call Christmas "Xmas". "It's like taking Christ away from Christmas!" they say. It's a reflection of the way Christmas has become separated from the birthday of Jesus Christ.

But let's think about it in another way. When I receive a letter with a row of Xs at the bottom, it tells me that the sender loves me very much.

When we see Christmas written "Xmas" it can remind us that God loves us so much that he sent his own Son to tell us. So Xmas starts with a big kiss to remind us of God's great love. And of course an X is a cross and Jesus' love took him all the way from the stable to the cross."

Judith Merrell

YOUTH

"Few things are more satisfying than seeing your children
have teenagers of their own."

Doug Larson

*"To an adolescent, there is nothing in the world more
embarrassing than a parent."*

Dave Barry

Mothers of teenagers know why animals eat their young!

You can tell a child is growing up when he stops asking you where he comes from and starts refusing to tell you where he's going.

"If you want to recapture your youth, just cut off his allowance."

Al Bernstein

"The best substitute for experience is being 16."

Raymond Duncan

"Little children: headache; big children: heartache."

Italian proverb

It rarely occurs to teenagers that the day will come when they'll know as little as their parents.

It is not what a teenager knows that bothers his parents; it is how he found out.

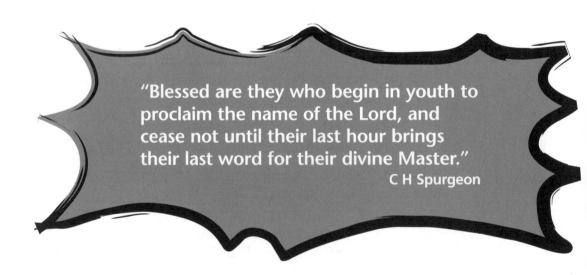

"Blessed are they who begin in youth to proclaim the name of the Lord, and cease not until their last hour brings their last word for their divine Master."

C H Spurgeon

Youngsters have to deal with mental health problems on a scale never previously recognised, new research reveals.

More than a third of young people know someone who has attempted suicide and 25% are worried about the mental health of a young person they know, according to the survey.

The research has been released to mark the launch of a new Department of Health campaign which aims to improve understanding of mental health issues amongst young people.

The survey showed young people's experience of mental health problems was far greater than previously realised.

Some 86% of the 1,001 15–21-year-olds surveyed knew someone who had experienced a mental health problem.

Just under half knew someone who had self-harmed, and 68% knew someone who had suffered depression.

Of those polled, 17% said they knew someone who had experienced schizophrenia.

Young women in particular knew of people with mental health problems – 93% compared to 79% of young men.

Although mental health issues appeared to be commonplace for young people, many felt there was ignorance and lack of information about the problem.

Health Minister Jacqui Smith said: "This new research reveals that the vast majority of young people need accessible, relevant information to help them deal with an issue about which they feel ill-informed."

ZEAL

There is a tale told of that great English actor, Macready. An eminent preacher once said to him: "I wish you would explain to me something." "Well, what is it? I don't know that I can explain anything to a preacher."

"What is the reason for the difference between you and me? You are appearing before crowds night after night with fiction, and the crowds come wherever you go. I am preaching the essential and unchangeable truth, and I am not getting any crowd at all."

Macready's answer was this: "This is quite simple. I can tell you the difference between us. I present my fiction as though it were truth; you present your truth as though it were fiction."

ZUSYA

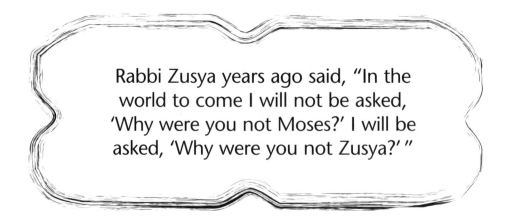

Rabbi Zusya years ago said, "In the world to come I will not be asked, 'Why were you not Moses?' I will be asked, 'Why were you not Zusya?'"

Index